The Boy
with a
Snake
in his
Schoolbag

The Boy
with a
Snake
in his
Schoolbag

A Memoir from Manila.
(Or Something Like That.)

Bob Ong
Illustrated by Freely Abrigo

TUTTLE Publishing

Tokyo | Rutland, Vermont | Singapore

For

Teachers
Students
Used to be students
Would rather not be students
Dropouts
Kick outs
Transferees
Cross-enrollees
and Honors Students

I have never let my schooling interfere with my education.
—MARK TWAIN

SECOND GRADE. SECTION ONE.[1] A day in June,[2] in a public elementary school. The small canteen was divided into two, one half serving as our classroom. We were about forty pupils. There were thirty-nine chairs; only thirty had all their parts. Nine young learners would have to make do with wobbly Frankenstein seats. One would have to play musical chairs every single school day. That kid was me.

A makeshift blackboard was the only thing between us and the gas stoves with bubbling soups cooked daily by designated teachers. It was in this room that we were given an assignment: bring a toy to class for our first Show and Tell. Hardly a problem for me since my father was a "seaman," which in the Philippines in the 1980s meant he worked on a ship somewhere far away and brought home imported goods, electronic equipment and relatively expensive toys good enough to be presented in class for academic purposes. I decided to bring an AA-battery-operated police car. It wasn't much, but I picked it for Show and Tell since it fitted easily in my small bag. I came prepared and I couldn't have prayed any harder for my name to be called. Luckily, just before I felt numbness in the arm that I kept raised for almost the entire period, my teacher finally noticed me.

---

1 Class of the best students (in theory!).

2 First month of the school year in the Philippines.

Probably because everybody had been called and I was the only volunteer left.

"ROBERTO!"

Eyes popped and jaws dropped when I walked to the front of the class. In my hands was nothing less than a battery-operated toy. In those days, most kids could only afford marbles. Anyone who had a toy that ran on batteries was a god.

"D-dis is my toy . . . eee-eeeets ah kar," I said nervously, in my best English.

"What kind of car, Roberto?" asked my teacher who for the first time in her life realized I existed in her class.

"Aah po-lis kar . . . eet has baterees . . ."

It was a resounding success. I won everybody's respect, became an instant celebrity and, by some miracle, finally had my own chair by the end of the day. It was glorious. Just before the school bell rang, my teacher hastily reminded everyone to bring another toy the following day. Great, I thought. More minutes of fame. I was so excited.

For the next round, I decided to bring a clown mask made of cheap plastic. Again, chosen for the sole reason that it fit in my school bag. It wasn't long before the entire class found out what I had and the excitement soon got out of hand. When the ruckus reached my teacher, I was summoned to explain what I had in my bag—after she slapped my thigh. Ouch.

"Y-you told us to bring . . . another toy, Ma'am . . ."

"Did I say anything like that?" she asked the entire class in a voice that guaranteed pain and suffering to anyone who said yes.

Nobody dared to respond. It still bothers me to this day when I wonder whether the instruction to bring another toy

8

was all imaginary or my classmates just unanimously decided I'd make a good burnt offering.

That was Miss Uyehara, my teacher. Small, old, single, with thick, black-rimmed glasses. Though a practice still acceptable at that time, I'm still not really sure why she slapped me. And it happened again many times—with other teachers, in many ways, in different years, in more academic institutions. I was in and out of schools for seventeen years. I've been a teacher's pet and a teacher's enemy, drawn cats and dogs with pencils and crayons, cheated in exams, borrowed notebooks, kept what I borrowed, volunteered in recitations, cleaned classrooms, cut classes, deliberately missed whole days of school, faked excuse letters, vandalized school property, attended proms, made it to the top ten in a national college assessment exam, signed yearbooks, wrote "I promise to bring my PE uniform" three hundred times, learned to march in citizen army training, earned a medal in quiz bee, topped and failed tests and attended flag ceremonies.

Seventeen years. I did learn some lessons along the way. And sometimes, it feels good to review them.

THE BEGINNING. FIRST GRADE, DAY ONE. This is the fun part—the start. All your stuff is brand new, except if you're someone like me with older siblings, then you're bound to have some hand-me-downs. But it sure feels amazing to write in a new *nokbook* (notebook) and use a store-fresh paper pad, ball pen, pencil, sharpener, eraser, pencil case, glue, scissors, ruler, crayons, art paper, *kokomban* (coupon bond a.k.a. writing paper), poster paper, manila envelopes, raincoat or umbrella, lunchbox, water jug and school bag—the more they smelled of factories the more awesome they were!

The pupil with the coolest stuff is always popular. Jealousy is acceptable and envy is normal, especially if some kids have a Sesame Street pencil case while others make do with a plastic pouch. Some students own candy-scented erasers, while others survive on a rubber band wrapped and knotted on a pencil's head. There are those whose lunch packs come in Tupperware sets and there are those who only have a small loaf of bread to pack. Some have imported backpacks and some get by with fishnets, the type used as a bag for buying market produce. Different children of different backgrounds—they're all present and peacefully coexisting in the academic melting pot called public school.

First grade is fun. Lots of cool stuff to discover. It's when I first learned to read a whole paragraph, write a full sentence and draw animals that didn't look like impressionist

paintings of cockroaches. In this class I also learned more poems and songs than ever before and how to count from one to a hundred. You can't beat the adrenaline rush from counting down from a hundred to one, or counting in tens, or in fives . . . real fast! As if counting is the solution to the world's problems.

"Bow-wow-wow!" barked Spot.
"Spot! Spot!" called Pepe. "Go catch the ball."
"Bow-wow-wow!" barked Spot.

This is what you'd typically read in books, in large print and bold typeface. Starting with abakada[3] (A, E, I, O, U; Ba, be, bi, bo, bu; ka, ke, ki, ko, ku . . .) then forming words (ba-ka, baka; ba-hay, bahay; ba-ba-e, babae[4]). I was able to impress my teacher once with my ability to read fast. But it ended abruptly when I read "cottage" as "house." She found out that I was just guessing the words based on pictures.

The ability to read is a serious matter though. It's an important rite of passage. A badge that says "literate." From here on, you can read the lies in newspapers, subtitles in foreign movies and the writing on vandalized bus seats such as "If you read this, you're stupid!"

Picture this: a thin book. Yellow cover. A picture of a woman sprawled on the floor, holding a book, teaching a boy and a girl who seem to enjoy learning. This is the age-old book of *Abakada* (First steps to reading), nothing else. This is how natural born Filipinos are initiated into literacy.

---

3 The Filipino alphabet.
4 The Filipino words for cow, house and woman.

We go through A-E-I-O-U and read *bao, bibi, baba; aso, baso, tasa; at puso, pusa, puno*,[5] again and again. The entire class in unison, reading loudly, slowly, every single day. We read. We write. We read.

I've no idea how long we've been benefiting from this book. But last time I looked at it, I discovered a high entertainment value I never noticed before, in sentences such as:

The bread tastes like pulp.
The noodle is moldy.
I want to eat a chick.
You and I will eat every day.
Have pity on the battered child.
There is a mad dog on the road.
Judas' kiss was bad.

The book is still in use today and judging from my nephew's copy, there seem to be no changes in its fate. Its pictures are still victims of the scrawls of crayons possessed by malevolent hands, colored in uneven strokes that go beyond the lines: puppies and carabaos are blue; the mother and the garlic green; a cat is red and blue, as if defaced by a junkie.

As years have passed, however, some developments have found their way onto the pages of the classic book. The Filipino alphabet has been updated. What once had twenty letters now has twenty-eight. Two more than the English alphabet. The letters C, F, J, Q, V, X, Z and Ñ have been added, which is a big deal. So words such as cab, jelly,

---

5 Basic Filipino words: coconut shell, duck, chin; dog, drinking glass, cup; heart, cat, tree.

España, quintuplet, Xerox, zodiac, visa and french fries are now included in the classic book of the Filipino alphabet. So cool to sound so first world.

Can you imagine texting, social media and E-mail if we never learned to read? Who could've guessed that it all started from the unassuming book of *Abakada*?

A E I O U
A B N K K B S K N P L
B K W L K M G W
P R M S Y T W K
H H H M S Y K N B
T W P H H H H H
O H L T M N
P R K N T Ng[6]

(A E I O U
Oh my! You can read now!
You probably don't have anything to do
It would be nice to laugh
Hahaha! Are you happy now?
Laugh some more, hahahahaha!
Okay, that's enough.
You look like a moron.)

---

6 Phonetically, the Filipino alphabet can sound like actual words. This set of letters, which parodies reading exercises for first graders, is a popular joke among kids in school.

IF YOU ASK FILIPINOS what their favorite subject in elementary school was, about half would answer "recess" in a heartbeat.

Now I'm not sure about private schools, but during my time in public school, recess was that one small window of opportunity for a child to stuff his gut with food rich in sugar, oil, additives, preservatives, MSG and—on some occasions—rancid carbohydrates and cholera.

The menu basically consisted of junk food five days a week, sold from a tray that was carried around the room. Things could get worse though, because the food tray reaching you empty was always a dreaded daily possibility. Didn't matter that our school nutritionist, if we ever had one, was probably just a five-year-old kid with brownish gums and jagged teeth . . . our food tray, with its cornucopia of edible scraps, was always emptied. Bless us, O Lord. Everything was sold and eaten. Every. Single. Day.

The Tray, which contained all the sweet and salty child-friendly carcinogens that nourished our little bodies every day, was actually an oversized baking pan, 3 inches (7.5 cm) deep and 1 x 2 feet (30 x 60 cm) wide. Two girls in each class, usually the same tandem every day, would peddle the products in The Tray around the room. If they started at the first row and you happen to be seated on the fourth row, you could kiss your recess goodbye as there would be

nothing left to buy. Good thing the system changed eventually, at least under the administration of progressive class teachers. The Tray started its rotation on different rows depending on the day of the week.

So, what exactly did The Tray contain? Cheese curls, potato chips, corn chips, *cornick* (deep-fried crunchy puffed corn), watermelon seeds, bubble gum, candies, chocolates and all sorts of junk food easily available in Filipino neighborhood stores. On rare occasions, options that offered some nutrition also found their way into The Tray: macaroni or spaghetti, boiled *saba* bananas, *nilupak* (mashed cassava), *puto* (rice cake), *kutsinta* (rice-based cake), *kalamay* (sticky rice-based cake) and *hopia* (bean-filled mooncake-like pastry). But, again, these relatively healthier and more filling Pinoy snacks were rarely available. And because the preparation was hardly industry standard, it was not uncommon that they reached you stale.

On some days when the teachers in charge of the school canteen felt like it, soup would also be available. You still couldn't trust the cleanliness of the utensils served with your order, but other than that, this steaming goodness was your best choice from the recess menu. Didn't matter that you would have to put up with a scalded tongue and dead tissue in your mouth after being forced to finish your boiling-hot soup in the space of five minutes.[7]

As for water, wimps could always bring their own in a plastic jug printed with cute cartoon characters. Otherwise,

---

7 Recess was for fifteen minutes; the soup would always be served ten minutes late.

you'd live on the wild side like everybody else in school and get yours directly from the outdoor faucet where the hose used to water the plants in the garden was attached. That's where I usually quenched my thirst, using bare hands placed under the spout as if drinking from a crystal-clear spring. I never really found out if I was drinking potable water or if my stomach had just learned to enjoy the company of amoebas.

Update: Implementing the Republic Act 8976 and the Department of Education Order No. 8, s. 2007, the Education Secretary has officially prohibited the use of MSG in food in public schools and the selling of junk food, carbonated drinks and artificial juices. Other than fresh juice, milk, shakes, fruits, vegetables, rice, corn and root vegetables, only fortified food products or ones with the official government seal will be allowed by the agency. In addition, the Department of Education also now requires the placement of the menu on the bulletin board of school canteens, listing the nutritional value of every food sold. Good news? I'm not so sure. I haven't stepped into any public elementary school in a very long time to know if this is being implemented. Some teachers I asked only responded with a giggle. At least things are funny, I guess.

NAH. FILIPINOS ARE JUST KIDDING when they say that their favorite subject in school is recess. Everybody knows nothing beats dismissal. Of course.

The frontage of a public elementary school instantaneously transforms into a medieval marketplace at the end of every school day. Food, toys, pets, what-have-yous— everything is up for sale. It's an entirely different world, where students buy something as they leave the gates. This was the shopping list:

- Fish balls
- *Tokneneng* (quail eggs covered in flour with orange food coloring)
- Hot dogs (in a bun, on a stick, waffle)
- Pancakes
- *Samalamig* (basically sweetened water with jelly and sago pearls, in different flavors, with occasional strands of human hair)
- Cotton candy
- Ice candy
- Ice cream
- Ice scramble (a shaved ice dessert)
- Ice water
- Tamarind, kerson fruit, java plums and other fruit snacks that go best with salt

- Jicama, cotton fruit, unripe mango and other fruit snacks that go best with shrimp paste
- *Tex* (playing cards), *jolen* (marbles), a s*ipa* ball for street games of kick volleyball)
- *Turumpo* (spinning top), *sumpit* (blowguns), yoyos
- Cheap plastic action figures and rubber balls
- Stickers and paper dolls
- Toy necklaces and bracelets
- Carts of Game & Watch and View Master rentals (granddaddies of portable video game consoles and VR headsets, respectively)
- And carts of chicks, ducklings, fish, birds and white mice sold as pets by lottery, yes, you read that right

My older sister's favorite was the Valentyme's Day necklace. It had a red heart-shaped pendant where your initial—subject to availability—was painted in white. Plus, it was made of chalk, so when you got tired of it you could use it to vandalize the walls at home.

My brother, on the other hand, would rather spend his allowance on the pet lottery, assuming he didn't spend everything on Nutribuns[8] (which he usually did, to gain the favor of his teachers). He did get lucky one time and brought home nine ducklings. Unfortunately, some rat got luckier, because only six duckling heads were left in the cage outside the house the following day.

There may be more stuff sold in front of public elementary schools these days. But I'm pretty sure there'd still be

---

8 Tastes like whole wheat bread that's about thirteen months past its expiration date.

young girls with beads of sweat on their noses, busy gnawing at green mangoes topped with shrimp paste and young boys still trying their hand at winning some ducklings. Because, really, life can be sour at times and rats may be everywhere, but taking chances is what it's all about.

DO YOU REALLY BELIEVE that the Earth is round and not flat? Are you sure? I'd say yes to both. Pretty sure.

Case in point: for me and my cousin Ally, being picked up from school by an adult relative, Monday to Friday, at five o'clock, was a set of facts as incontrovertible as the Earth being round. Except it didn't happen one time. And the Earth, suddenly, was flat.

Class had just ended. We were looking in the direction of the people at the classroom door: huddled parents and guardians, ready to fetch their kids at the teacher's signal. No familiar face was in sight that day, however. No problem, we thought, maybe they've just been blocked from view. We were confident. Until everyone had left and we were the only pupils remaining in the room. We decided to leave the building and that was when we found out what was waiting for us. A rumbling, tempestuous, pissed-off rain. The kind that could float Noah's boat.

For a reason only seven-year-olds can probably explain, we decided we would walk home by ourselves. Most likely this was my idea because I was never comfortable waiting and doing nothing. My cousin had a Hello Kitty umbrella which we shared. It was cute and had it been any smaller, you'd mistake it for a mushroom.

We had two options going home. One route was a major road that passed through a street that was always so flooded it might as well have been the Ganges. The other route was a dusty road during summer and a muddy marsh in monsoon season. We opted for the Ganges. Wrong move. The water was too deep and there was stuff floating in it that seemed to have come out of people's digestive tracks.

No choice. We resorted to "mud land." My cousin is not a Filipino and her family had just moved to the Philippines. I was fully aware that she was my responsibility. So, it was very traumatic, to say the least, to hear her scream an incomprehensible "Chuchee! Chuchee!" when she stepped on a piece of swampy trash with her black velvet shoe.

It wasn't a short trip, but we did reach home eventually. With only a small patch of hair on our heads remaining dry and black mud stuck on our shoes so thick we could make clay pots out of it. But we didn't die, so I guess it was all good.

But this wouldn't be the first time that no one came to meet us. The next time it happened, we did exactly the same thing. Only it wasn't raining. In a game of chicken, we dared each other to climb the footbridge over a busy road. We didn't need to cross the road, we were just after the thrill of being up so high and then we would run back down the same steps we had climbed. As always, it was probably my idea. But I suffered a historic loss in the game of chicken the day my uncle who came to pick us up from school found us on the footbridge we had no business using. It took weeks before I heard the end of my mother's lectures.

That was pretty much my mission statement in grade school: to walk through the flood despite the mud when it rains and go up a bridge when the sun is up no matter the cost, as the journey will bring you back home, is fun and is always worth it.

I WILL NEVER FORGET how my classmates and I fought over who got to do the errand for my third-grade class adviser.[9] She needed a dozen Nutribuns for the other teachers. In elementary school, students who get to do stuff for teachers are superstars. They're automatically promoted to the level of jail warden, excused from classroom activities and are instant teachers' pets.

I luckily got picked that day. Class dismissal was at twelve noon.[10] I was allowed to leave the classroom at eleven thirty for the task. Unfortunately the canteen was busy that day with long queues at the counter. Tick . . . eleven forty . . . tock . . . eleven fifty . . . the line was hardly moving. The teachers assigned to the counter were working painfully slowly—mostly just talking, engrossed in each other's life stories. I was about to lose it, especially when my classmate came into the canteen to hand over my school bag. The class had been dismissed. Everybody was already free while I was stuck doing an errand that was no longer serving me a purpose. Real bummer.

---

9 Homeroom teacher.
10 Classes only last half a day. There are two shifts to accommodate all students. This time I'm in the morning class.

It was one of the worst feelings in the world. To be left behind. I hated running out time during exams[11] and I abhor being the last one to leave a place.[12]

I felt like I was already in a different dimension by half past midday. The familiar faces of students from the morning shift were all gone and had been replaced by those in the afternoon classes. Strangers.

I came home with a long face and was mad at the world. My Teacher's Pet Theory had backfired. I felt like I had just lost a decade of my life to the weevil-infested buns that didn't even taste good. It was the last-known time I volunteered to fulfill any teacher's wish list.

---

11 The pressure sucks.
12 Especially school.

WIPING THE BLACKBOARDS, sweeping the floor, mopping the floor, applying wax to the floor and polishing it by foot using coconut husks, watering the plants and taking out the garbage daily—these were all tasks carried out by students in a public school where the one or two janitors only have time to clean the principal's office and a few other revered rooms. The school building's maintenance and cleanliness were the responsibility of the students. We were all expected to be independent, mindful, neat and always orderly. To make sure the library was kept quiet and clean, its use was never encouraged. Oftentimes, it was even prohibited. I'm not sure we ever had a librarian, much less a school nurse or clinic. The only time we were able to enter and stay in the library was when our classrooms were being used for PTA meetings and we were forced out.

In first grade, every day after recess the boys would form a line along the school's perimeter wall to pee. The girls, on the other hand, did their business in a grassier spot. In second grade, we had a plastic bucket behind the door inside the classroom where you could relieve yourself. This portable toilet, Miss Uyehara's brainchild, was devised to outwit the boys who took too many bathroom breaks. But I can now admit to the times I purposely missed the bucket so it wouldn't overflow. I had such a debilitating fear of Miss

Uyehara that I would rather pee on the floor than risk the bucket overflowing while she was teaching.

We did have restrooms in school back then, but again, there were no janitors to maintain them. So, anyone who went in would definitely take a puke before taking a dump. Even if you had diarrhea, you'd shy away. And because nobody could stomach to use the facilities, it wasn't uncommon for our comfort rooms' reputation to be shrouded in supernatural urban legends. While it was an established fact that our toilets did smell of rotten corpse, I don't believe our school was a former graveyard. What I do support, though, is the theory that these narratives originated in the minds of students who had to create stories to distract themselves from diarrhea.

OTHER THAN A HALF-DAY CLASS and frequent suspension of classes, there were more perks in elementary
school. When boredom became unbearable, for instance,
you could just pray for a random visitor to come by, which
was a good opportunity to put to use what your teacher had
taught you for the occasion. The classic greeting, in chorus
was: "Goooood mooorning, viiiiisiiitohr!"[13]

We often had "surprise guests." It wasn't uncommon for
a whole period to go to waste because representatives from
a popular publisher of children's books were allowed to take
over the class and talk about the books they were selling.
Other times it was a representative from NEDA[14] with a free
and on-the-spot crash course on handicrafts, as a ploy to sell
DIY materials for pincushions, Christmas decorations, wo-
ven baskets and other projects that were fun, challenging
and definitely more suitable for people older than us and
serving a sentence in jail. Salesmen of just about any product
were allowed to interrupt the class, selling metal polish, floor
wax, cleaning products, biscuits, reference books or model-
ing clay. On not so rare occasions, even visitors who weren't
selling anything, just flat out asking for money, were also
allowed in class, requesting donations for victims of flood
or fire, or for a sick family member, or a dying relative, or a

---

13 Syllables are always lengthened to achieve unison.
14 The National Economic and Development Authority.

dead neighbor. Sometimes with accompanying pictures that haunted us for many years. In addition to this, there were various school organizations asking us to buy fund-raising raffle tickets or make cash donations to the school for the popularity contest on United Nations Day, where the candidates who pooled the biggest amounts won the title of Mr. and Ms. UN. All these in a free-for-all stickup.

On good days,[15] though, we also got given product samples. I had a blast when the Crest team arrived one time and gave away packs containing a toothbrush, toothpaste and plaque disclosing tablets. I was so excited I managed to brush my teeth seven days in a row.

In what was probably another money-making venture, because tickets were sold, I was also lucky enough to watch a film—not an educational documentary, but a blockbuster movie. The school administration simply detached the partitions of around eight classrooms to create a hall, brought in a projector and turned on the electric fans that were somehow still working and . . . voilà! We had an instant sweat-scented cinema.

With or without visitors, though, regular classes or not, everyone in school knew how to pass time when the day just seemed unbearable. Here are some of the things we did:

Game: SOS
Players: 2
Materials: Pen and paper
Rules: Familiar with tic-tac-toe? Just draw more boxes and instead of using letters X and O, use letters S and O to

---

15 We did have some.

32

form sequences of S-O-S. First to make ten, or a hundred, depending on boredom, wins.

Game: Spin-A-Win
Players: 2
Materials: Pen and paper
Rules: Basically, Wheel of Fortune on paper. Categories can be person, place, thing or event. Players take turns guessing the letters of the opponent's mystery word. First to guess wins.

Game: F.L.A.M.E.S.
Player: 1
Materials: Pen, paper, hidden desires
Rules: Write down your full name. Write down your crush's full name below yours. Cross out the common letters your names share. Total the number of leftover letters in each of your names. Your total reflects your feelings for your crush. Your crush's total reflects his or her feelings for you. Then you add your totals together. The sum predicts your future as a couple. FLAMES has six letters. Simply count where your number lands for your own total and your combined total. F stands for friendship, L is for love, A is for anger, M is for marriage, E for engagement and S is for sweetheart. If your total is more than six, just go back to F and continue counting. It's a cute and popular childish game but one I'm not so fond of after my name added up to love, my crush's totaled to angry and together it was marriage but she's now happily married to a Japanese guy who owns the club she works at overseas.

Game: War

Players: 2

Materials: Pen, paper, detergent soap

Rules: Each player draws their soldiers on either end of a piece of paper; this end is your base. Soldiers can be of any equal number and represented by any symbol (e.g., ten soldiers for each player; yours are circles, your opponent's are triangles.) First player moves by placing the tip of an upright pen on any of their soldiers and putting their index finger on the other end of the pen. Using the index finger, player quickly pushes the pen so the tip creates a skid mark toward their opponent's base. Any soldier from the opponent's base that gets hit by the skid mark is eradicated and crossed out. First to finish off the opponent's soldiers wins. Players then use the detergent soap to wash the ink stains out of their school uniform.

Game: War II

Players: 2

Materials: Pen, paper, cash

Rules: Same as War, but a bit messier. To move, draw a small circle within your base and color it with a pen. Now fold the paper in half and look for the circle you just colored in on the other side of the paper. Rub it using the cap of a pen so that the heavily shaded circle can make a mark on your opponent's base. Any soldier the shading hits is eradicated. First to finish off the opponent's soldiers wins. Use the cash to buy a new pen to replace your inkless and now useless old pen.[16]

---

16 May still be upcycled as a drinking straw; there's probably a tutorial on YouTube.

Game: Spirit of the Coin

Players: 2–4

Materials: Coin, sheet of paper—ideally A4 or bigger

Rules: Ouija, but with a coin. When bored, use the coin to play heads or tails.

Game: Spirit of the Pen

Players: 2

Materials: Two pens (those types with a hole at the end)

Rules: Ouija, but with a pen. Each player will hold a pen horizontally, with the tip of one pen inserted into the hole of the other. Meditate and call up a spirit. Ask a question answerable by yes or no. If the pens rise at the joint, the answer is yes. If the joint falls, the answer is no. If no movement is observed, the spirits have abstained. Move on to another game and leave dead politicians in peace.

There are other games that can be played inside the classroom, such as paper airplanes and other origami. But these get tiresome pretty quick and usually only result in crumpled papers everywhere by recess.

You are to travel from point A to point B and return. On the trip from A to B, you travel at thirty miles per hour. How fast would you have to travel from B to A in order to average sixty miles per hour for the round trip?

I REALLY DON'T KNOW WHY I've always despised math. Since kindergarten, statements from my teacher like "one apple plus one apple . . ." already put me to sleep. I wasn't aware that it was math then; all I knew was I never had any interest in it. Whenever the lesson seamlessly shifted into that, I would just stare at the posters of the alphabet in the room, from A to Z, then back to A, again and again till my teacher was done with counting the ingredients for her fruit salad. Before I knew it, the class had already moved on to singing "If you're happy and you know it clap your hands . . ."

I experienced a cataclysm when I was in sixth grade. Since I belonged to the class of supposedly the best students, a teacher due for evaluation chose us as her "demo class." I entered the room that day and was greeted by a collage of art papers in the shape of a tree posted on the blackboard. On its branches were cardboard geometric fruits with a math problem written on the back which we were supposed to answer. And the tree of mathematical problems probably smelled my fear because my name was called early on. I was trembling as I walked to the board and picked my fruit. I will forever remember my dread and uncertainty while deciding on a medium-sized orange pentagon. It turned out to be a multiplication problem that I couldn't answer.[17] I badly wanted to stick it back on the tree right away, but all eyes were already on me—those of my forty classmates, class adviser, the teacher being evaluated, the school principal, the school's division superintendent and a few other teachers who probably only wanted to be excused from their own classes. I was having cold sweats and my throat was parched. The forty-two seconds I spent motionless in front of the class felt like a hundred years. Nobody tried to supply an answer. In my mind I had already prayed to all the angels and saints, but none gave me a hint. I only came to when I finally heard the voice of the teacher who robbed me of all my dignity: "Okay, class, so who would like to help Roberto?"

On that day, I officially condemned mathematics to the status of heart disease. And since then, I have never ever forgotten the answer to that painful math problem. Keep this in mind at all times: 8 x 7 = 56.

✐ ✎ ✐

The experience made me wonder for a very long time. Why, of all subjects, did my school decide to have the teachers who feast on children handle math classes? My teacher in fifth grade, for instance, would always play mathematics jingles on her portable cassette player in class. She prob-

---

17 There were only very few multiplication problems that I could answer.

ably wanted us to memorize the multiplication table and other mathematical information while enjoying playful and catchy melodies. But none of us students liked the music—all we could hear were our nervous heartbeats whenever we shared the room with her. Probably because every time you gave an incorrect answer to a quiz or recitation, her curly hair would morph into little snakes, her eyes shoot death rays and her thundering voice break icebergs in the North Pole. She was definitely responsible for making us abhor math even more.

I kept thinking, if the alphabet can form equations ($c = a + b$), why couldn't numbers make a sentence ("32 asked 4,150 if 7 will 59 8")? Is there truth in the theory that Satan himself dared God to allow algebra in the world to test man's faith through utter pain and sorrow? And who on earth is X? How could he be so foolish that he's always lost and needs to be found? He even has Y tagging along with him on some occasions. Doesn't matter how careful or mindful you are, they always run away and go missing. And regardless of your innocence in the incident, the burden of looking for them always rests on you. All that math knows and all that it is good for is in giving you orders while it sits on its throne and scratches its bottom: Find! Solve! Simplify! And fix me a cup of coffee, you worthless piece of Pi!

Why should the entire class look for the value of each letter? "You won't believe the good news that you're about to hear, Ma'am, but my classmate here, Archimedes Pythagoras Newton Jr., finally found X and we can all breathe easier now!" That kid is a math wizard, he always finds the value of X; isn't that enough? Would the value change if I looked for X myself? Is it my obligation to solve math's own problems? Why? Would it help to lower my Internet bill if I factor a quadratic trinomial? Would the Laws of Exponents solve Earth's problems with plastic pollution? Would the Associative Law of Multiplication lower our country's crime rates? Would it benefit a couple to learn the sum and difference of two cubes? Would parallelograms, polynomials and cotangents be good for blood circulation? Do we really need to put up with irrational numbers?

In its defense, though, I do believe that math is a universal language. There's math in arts, music, science and sports. Time and space are math. A watch, calendar, map, money and the globe are all math. Length, distance, speed, size, quantity, height, volume, weight, width, depth and shape—these are all math. As are the Rubik's Cube, Pacman, Monopoly, Lego, the lottery, jigsaw puzzles, the piano, dominoes, dice, roulette, playing cards, financial statements, elections, the human body, pyramids, the Titanic, the Olympic Games, Mount Everest and the solar system.

The $17-billion Channel Tunnel under the English Channel seabed between England and France is also math; 31 miles 53 yards (50 km) in length and 24 feet 11 inches (7.5 m) in diameter; included in the *Guinness World Records* as the longest undersea tunnel, along with the MGM Grand Hotel with 5,005 rooms as the biggest hotel and the CN Tower with a height of 1,815 feet 5 inches (555 m) as the tallest building in the world. All included in *Guinness 2000*. All math.

From crossing the street to erecting buildings and starting a business, most decisions we make each day are based on math.

So, when you're all by yourself in a pizza parlor, don't slice a pizza into eight pieces because that's just too much for one person to eat. And if you buy lemons priced at fifty cents each, haggle first to see if you can buy three for two pesos instead. That's mathematics.

If your answer to the math problem at the start of this story is 90 mph, you're wrong. And that is basically the reason I hate math.

I still have my math notebook from first grade to day. On its cover is a label where I have handwritten: "Mafhemafics."

The first page has the badly written numbers 0 to 5, repeated over and over again. The 2s look like question marks and the 3s resemble butterflies, with lots of obvious erasures and corrections.

There are also drawings of different objects inside a box. We would count the objects and write down the number beside the box. It was a do-it-yourself system of answering an activity sheet which we ourselves created. A workbook was unheard of back then. I did accomplish the activity and there's a big red check mark across the page of the notebook and a score that says "100." Perfect.

On the next two pages are the handwritten numbers 1 to 50, and 51 to 100. From the looks of it, I'd bet the entire thing took three days to finish. The succeeding pages contain more count-the-objects-inside-the-box activity, with different objects drawn: vertical lines, X marks, circles, triangles, balloons, lollipops, carts, tops, slingshots, yoyos, trees, apples, buttons, stones, shells and some DNA or sperm cells, I can't tell. Apparently, all we did in class was count anything you see on this planet.

A lesson on currency was also covered, as well as roman numerals, fractions ("one whole, one holf, one third, one fourd"), days of the week, months of the year and telling the time. No other lesson followed "How to Tell the Time." The next pages of the notebook are blank. It was probably enough to learn that the hands of the clock move forward and so does time.

That math notebook is unbelievable. Everything in it was written by my seven-year-old hand. Every stroke of pencil and mark of eraser. The design on its cover is a picture of a young boy with a long, golden, 1970s haircut, holding a walking stick. Beside him are bold letters that say "Let's go on!"

MY SCHOOL BAG IN FIRST GRADE had the words Cathay Pacific printed on it. It looked like an oversized green coin purse with one big pocket on the side and a narrow strap. Couldn't be any simpler. A bag. Just that. Probably a legit souvenir item, brought home by my father after a trip, but could also be just another thoughtless design my mom bought mindlessly from a sidewalk vendor. "Wow, an oversized green coin purse with one big pocket on the side, a narrow strap and the words Cathay Pacific printed on it! My son would definitely love this!"

I put all my test papers in the big pocket and intentionally carried the bag the wrong way, inwards, with the side pocket and Cathay Pacific close to my body and hidden from view. My brother asked why I carried my bag like a cretin. When I explained that it was so thieves couldn't steal from me, he just laughed. I couldn't blame him. He had no idea how much drawings marked "very good" and "100%" cost on the black market.

✏ ✐ ✎

There were days when the responsibility of fetching me from school rested on my big sister. One time she made me stand just outside our classroom as she inspected my bag. She said we weren't going home till she was done tidying

43

it up. The reason being that every school day by five thirty my bag had become an instant landfill of pages torn from paper pads, loose sheets of unused paper, crumpled paper, art paper, art paper cuttings, scissors, spilled glue, glue caps, toothpaste, toothbrush, bath soap, comb, damp face towel, pencil, half of what used to be an eraser, the other half of what used to be an eraser, my classmate's eraser which somehow found its way into my bag, my classmate's crayons, my own crayons mostly broken in two, the *Abakada* book, two to three more textbooks, place mat, biscuits, the Chuck Norris of pastries a.k.a. Nutribun and a snake.

"What on earth is this? You even have a snake in your bag!" she annoyingly asked, to which I could only reply with a big grin. In my defense, though, it was just a twenty-inch (50-cm) rubber snake. And to be fair to the seven-year-old me, I am not going to try to speak on his behalf. It's been four decades now and I have no idea whatsoever of what could have possibly come to that kid's mind at that point in history. What I can offer, however, is an explanation for all the toiletries: we were required to bring these as our "grooming and cleanliness" kit. Didn't matter that we never took a bath nor brushed our teeth in school, which makes me doubt forty years later if my teacher's instruction to pack a bathroom was a daily requirement or a one-time thing, particularly the one about the face towel having to be damp, which was probably why my bag always smelled of mold.

✎ ✏ ✐

Unlike my Cathay Pacific bag which had no inner compartments and could be easily mistaken for a food blender with its mixed contents, my khaki bag in second grade had more pockets than a carpenter's vest. Unfortunately, with all the bells and whistles in the upgrade, durability might have been compromised a bit which led to the bag getting torn apart for unknown reasons barely a month into the new school year. I will never forget what we went through, though . . .

I was probably already outgrowing my school shorts on the day I suddenly decided to jump out of a running public jeep on my way home instead of getting off properly, which I usually did. The action was close to how one would jump from a plane in a skydive. It was in that moment that I felt the world change. Beyond any doubt. In those days whenever I ran out of fresh briefs to put on in the morning, I just didn't bother and would go commando to school. And it was when I jumped off the jeep that I realized my poor choices in life. My shorts got ripped at the seams, instantly exposing what undergarments keep private. It didn't help that in the 1980s, shorts were accurately self-descriptive. Short. Unlike today's fashion when shorts can be repurposed as pillow cases. What saved me from embarrassment? My khaki backpack which covered my behind, working together with my hands which were covering my front. I had to walk down the street like a newly circumcised boy,[18] wearing shorts that were now little more than a loin cloth.

✐ ✉ ✎

It is both surprising and amusing to realize that I can still recall most of my school bags: from my Cathay Pacific and

---

18 Circumcision is customary for Filipino boys around puberty.

khaki bags, to the handbags, trolley bags, backpacks, satchels and binders that succeeded. More than their best friend or seatmate in class, students are in the constant company of their school bags, which also serve as a pillow or seat depending on how long the class takes, the number of school activities, the duration of a practice, how late one will be picked up or how bad the traffic is. Parents often remind their kids "take care of your belongings." But in the heart of a concerned loved one, there's that unspoken wish for the bag to "take care of my little one."

I still have with me today the last backpack I used in high school. It still has the patch of gummy dirt stuck to the bottom which I never got around to cleaning. Our bags got dirty easily because we would leave them just anywhere whenever we had an activity outside the classroom. We as a class would pile our belongings together in one place so it was easy to mind them; and only the bottoms of the bags got grimy because we usually placed them leaning against one another so that they didn't fall over. It was a common-sense approach that we were used to. It's usually only in schools that you witness such solidarity in possessions. In the real world, people rely on high walls to protect properties.

I see children's bags these days that resemble luggage. Too big and too heavy for their size and age. I am not sure if this means we are capable of learning so much more now or that our ignorance is getting worse.

A pleasant possession is useless without a comrade.
—SENECA

IF YOU WERE GIVEN A CHANCE to become a billion-aire but you would lose your family, friends, even acquain-tances and would never find the love of your life, would you say yes? What if you were given all the money in the world but every person on earth would disappear and you alone would remain, would you still say yes?

As a child, I would have definitely said yes to this. I re-member wishing that I could live in a mall so I'd have all the toys and ice cream that I wanted. I used to play by myself as a young kid, so I was pretty sure I wouldn't mind if all the other children on earth would disappear. If people were wiped out, no one would be stealing from anybody, there would be no bickering and totally no wars. And that would be so cool. Living in a mall would be just like living in the Garden of Eden with air conditioning!

Things changed at the end of my third grade, however. Because it was March[19] and the air already smelled of vaca-tion, my mother tolerated me not going to school every day. And I liked it. Except one day, a classmate in my neighbor-hood came by with a note from my teacher. I knew it could only be bad news. I was guilty.

---

19 The last month of the school year.

49

My mother, with a face that said "Oh, boy, you're in trouble!" opened the note with me. True enough, my teacher wanted me to be in school. The next day. Early. And it was very important that I comply.

I did report to school the following day—in my usual multicolored rubber shoes, with my usual multicolored socks, slightly faded blue shorts, white shirt and school ID. Basically a complete uniform. I saw other students on the way to school that day, but they were in polished black shoes, white socks, ironed skirt and blouse for girls and *barong* button-down shirt for boys, with fresh and neat haircuts, a hint of perfume, a garland of jasmine around their neck and accompanied by at least one family member who was just as well dressed. All this could only mean one thing.

It was Recognition Day. And I was one of the students who was going to receive an award. My teacher either wanted to surprise me or intentionally withheld the news to spite me for my absenteeism. Either way, it worked.

I had no time to go back home to alert my mother. And there were no public phones that I could use to call her. When I found my cousin in school, I begged her to go to our house and tell my mother to come immediately.

My mom didn't make it in time.

It was already my turn to come up to the stage. When my name was called, a mother came and pinned my award ribbon to my shirt. No, not my mother, who was nowhere to be found, but my classmate's mother, who surely felt sorry for me. And it was sad. That was probably the saddest sixty seconds of my young life. I didn't have a family, friend or even a relative with me. It would've been nice to see them happy for me, and seeing them happy for me would've made me really happy. But it was just me and success on the stage at that time. And it felt so worthless.

All the awards had been handed out and the ceremony finally came to an end. Still, my mother wasn't around. Had she known in time that her youngest child was to receive an honor, she'd definitely have had her hair permed in a neighborhood beauty parlor, mine trimmed most neatly in a corner barbershop, a decent shirt bought so I'd look good in pictures and one of my siblings yanked to go with her and clap for me.

Finally, just before everyone had left the school grounds, I saw my mother. It was easy to spot her from afar because of her floral umbrella. She was grinning and probably already knew what happened. I on the other hand was understandably pissed. She easily found a photographer who was still roaming around and had him take our picture. Weeks later, we received the photograph. She had a beautiful big smile in the picture. I had my eyes closed.

YOU CAN'T AVOID A STORM, not even inside a classroom.

The sun was shining brightly that day. The leaves on the trees were swaying most gently and the birds were jamming as they always do. Our teacher was preoccupied with the ordinariness of life and her lesson. It was the usual sunny good morning. Until the sun disappeared.

The class went on, a little better than before even, since the weather had cooled down. But then big heavy clouds started to cover the sky, which I was aware of because I was looking out the window and not at our teacher. That was when I also witnessed big drops of rain start falling. My teacher spoke louder so the noise wouldn't drown out her voice. And she almost succeeded. The noise the rain was making on the tin roof wouldn't have bothered us if the roof wasn't leaking. But our teacher, being a pro, simply took out the pail we used to water the garden and placed it under the hole to catch the drops of water. Done. Easy peasy.

We enjoyed about five minutes of peace. I knew our valiant teacher somehow felt relieved, as she did her best to hide her own fear and embarrassment. But nobody realized the heavens were just prepping for the final assault.

Suddenly a strong wind blew through our big capiz windows[20] and rain pelted into our classroom. We were officially

---

20 A classic type of window used in Filipino colonial architecture, also known as exotic windowpane oyster panels.

code red. The lesson was halted as we quickly ran to shut our door and what was left of the windows. Our teacher paused to consider her next move, as though she was playing chess.

But the enemy would not wait for its opponent.

In an instant, the rogue storm escalated to a Category 5. A ravaging wind and rain suddenly blasted our classroom. BAGAAAAAM! Our windows flew open, the bulletin board at the back of the classroom came off, the parts of the wall made of light wood broke apart. It was so violent I thought I heard the tempest cry: "CHAAAAAARGE!"

Luckily, we didn't get drenched as we would always run to a safe corner every time the storm surged. But our room wasn't as fortunate. All our artworks on display got soaked, including maps, charts and visual aids. Everything was wet. Not even our poster of Different Types of Weather was spared.

Because it was the apocalypse and our classroom was melting like chocolate, I knew my teacher was close to losing it and was about to expose her superhero identity by summoning her powers in front of the class. But she had no alter ego. Instead, she asked everyone to evacuate to the next room, which was a sound move till we met the class next door evacuating to our room. So, we opted to stay together and just weather the weather inside our room, with arms across the walls for support, hoping they didn't fall on us or fly away.

Minutes seemed to last forever, but the calamity did finally end. We survived, got ourselves dried, made it home in one piece and were able to go back to school the next day. But we had been moved to a different classroom. The one in the new building that had been finished just weeks before.

ACCORDING TO STUDIES, mental development mostly takes place in our first decade after being born. This is also the time of rapid learning. That is why it is also a major disadvantage to be deprived of education at this age. Or worse, to be uninterested in learning.

That was what set me and my buddy apart from the other kids. We did have our bickering, but we were partners in crime most of the time, particularly when it came to discovering the world. We found it cool to learn new things, especially stuff about science. And it was around this time that we discovered some reproductive-health literature that belonged to my sister who was in high school. What we learned about menstruation was mind-blowing. Like, for real?! So that was what that TV commercial for Stay Free was really about? Yuuuck. Our uncircumcised eight-year-old selves were disgusted—and amazed!

We simply couldn't take our minds off the illustration of the female reproductive system which we saw for the first time. Holy smokes, Batman, the thing had horns! And was that the baby factory? Whoa! Information overload. And the cross-section diagram of a male reproductive system was even more incredible! Like, that was what would become of our weenies? Seriously? Nothing could have prepared us for what we read: birth control, testes, puberty, eggs, family planning, ovaries, contraceptives, fallopian tubes, vas deferens, pills, uterus, urethra, ejaculatory duct, sterilization and the most important vocabulary we learned that day—vasectomy!

A few days later, a local government-sponsored circumcision program was held in the neighborhood. Despite their fears, curious boys ran to the town hall to see for themselves how it was done and to get it over with. And because my buddy was a natural show-off like me and wanted everybody in the street to know that we knew—unlike the other kids—what the actual medical procedure is called in English, he shouted in front to our house to call me.

"Bo-ob! Let's go have our VASECTOMY!"

There were two things we learned that day: one, it wasn't called vasectomy; two, "homeschooling" wasn't for us.

ON MY FIRST DAY in my first year, I was so nervous. My first friend in first year was Ronald Gonzaga. The first time we talked on the first day was on our first period class . . .

SMOTHERED IN "FIRST." This was a composition by my brother who grew up bingeing on Nutribun. It was part of their formal writing activity in English 1. My sisters and I had a good laugh the first time we read his masterpiece. And this story still comes up whenever the family gets together and we recall our funniest moments.

My case was a little bit different, though. My first day in high school was far from funny.

High school was totally different from elementary. I experienced culture shock. It was easy to tell that the other students in the academy were well off, unlike many of my friends in public elementary school whom I suspected had already quit the education system after our graduation.

Students in high school were very different from one another. Some were obviously half-wits from their looks alone. Others looked like geeks who know the Periodic Table of Elements by heart. Some looked like models who had probably already appeared in TV commercials, while some had too many zits—they looked like pimples that grew a face. Others were too sociable—you could tell they were aiming for the Student Council. And some were the classic snobs who acted like they were kids of a congressman and a mayor.

Even the teachers seemed different. Many looked young and cool and were probably not into Nutribuns. The classrooms looked better and seemed to be more durable and capable of withstanding the type of violent storm that ravaged our rickety school building in third grade. There were more facilities and the restrooms and library all seemed functional. The atmosphere was just different. High school was totally different.

✐ ✐ ✎

In elementary, you have a subject called Good Manners and Right Conduct that teaches just that. In high school, you have Regulations and Rules of Conduct that teaches a lesson for anyone who hasn't already learned enough:

- Cheating, forgery, vandalism and offensive behavior are prohibited
- A prescribed haircut, complete uniform and ID are required
- Gambling, physical abuse, defamation and indecent conduct are prohibited
- Attendance and punctuality in class and at flag ceremony are required
- And cigarette-smoking, as well as alcohol and drug use, possession of weapons and theft and damage to school property are—you guessed it right—prohibited

There was a set of rules for absences, school uniform and tests and examinations. Another set concerned conduct during flag ceremony, or when in the comfort room, canteen, library, clinic, school grounds, inside the classroom or even outside when there were inter-school activities.

Every offense had a penalty: reprimand, civic action, three-day suspension, five-day suspension, dismissal, and outright failure and disqualification for honors students.

The law professor Grant Gilmore once said, "The better the society, the less law there will be. In heaven there will be no law . . . in hell there will be nothing but law, and due process will be meticulously observed."

High school is hell.

Cool.

APART FROM BEING TOO YOUNG, grade schoolers couldn't go to the mall because there were no shopping malls near elementary schools back then. That's why in high school, I grabbed the chance to go to a popular nearby mall right away. Of course, it didn't end well.

I was with my classmate Head, as the class called him on account of him being short and with a big head, resembling a comic character of the same name. We were buddies and shared jeepney rides and always went home together right after class. Except that one time when we decided to go to the mall. I can no longer recall whose idea it was.

I don't think any amount of disguise would have worked to convince anyone that we were already "grown-ups." We were barely in our teens and what gave us away was the part of the mall we made a beeline for. The toy section. My efforts to act mature were wasted with Head gasping and wowing at every toy he saw. A lollipop and balloon couldn't have made him look more childish.

The trip would've made the day of the toddler I'd brought along if only the toy truck behind us hadn't fallen from the shelf.

PAAAGH!

There were just two things on my mind: Uh. Oh.

There was damage. A small chip on the funnel of the toy cement-mixer construction truck. A saleslady immediately approached, asked a couple of questions and nonchalantly took us to the store manager. We were escorted to the basement of the building where we passed by the employees' lounge. The place looked like a dungeon in my mind because it was underground and didn't look anything like the mall. I knew what everybody who saw us was thinking. Shoplifters! In high-school uniform. Uh. Oh.

I was quiet the entire time. The denial stage. Actuating an out of body experience. Head, in contrast, was optimistic, upbeat, hyper, high. I remember staring at the calendar in the office of the manager. It was my mother's birthday. While my siblings were probably busy preparing for the occasion at home, I was doing time in some manager's office. Barely a month into my new school. While the other freshmen were busy trying to attract attention and make good first impressions, I was in an underground cell. Depressed and suicidal.

Head and the manager reached an agreement. The dang truck would be paid for. But since we didn't have any money, Head asked if we could go back to school to get our class adviser's help. The manager had us leave our school bags as collateral.[21]

Unfortunately, our adviser was no longer on campus when we returned. But Head, my optimistic, upbeat, hyper buddy never lost hope, even at that point, which was both admirable and weird. He suggested we might as well pay our adviser a visit at her home, mere walking distance from the school. We probably knocked on around ten doors before finally getting the right one. As soon as our adviser opened

---

21 Make no mistake, this is a true story.

her door, Head started sniffling, which quickly progressed into quiet crying, before escalating to weeping and finally exploding into one big bad howl, all in about ten seconds. Finally admitting that somebody grabbed his lollipop and popped his balloon.

Our adviser was furious after she heard what happened. She wasted no time and stormed through the mall to lecture the manager. Eventually dues were paid and we left the place, with our heads held high thanks to this teacher who defended our juvenile dignity. Or so we thought.

The following day, our adviser asked me to stand in front of the class and tell the whole story, to serve as a lesson.

IF WE UNDERGO PHYSICAL CHANGES throughout elementary school, things get worse in high school. Much worse. And the zit is Public Enemy Number One. Nothing was more embarrassing than a *zyst*,[22] which is the combined force of abscessed zit, cyst, boil, wars and famine and all things ugly in the world. Right there on your face. Usually at the tip of your nose. Making you Rudolph minus the ability to guide a magical sleigh. And that's assuming you're lucky, because things could be worse—you could have acne that leaves you with a face full of holes, making people think you're a breathing cheese grater. So bad that a make-up artist would only need ketchup to cast you in *Night of the Living Dead*. That—in addition to a tacky school uniform, prescribed crew cut for boys and a pubertal voice that intermittently squeals, cracks and croaks—conspires to make you the most unattractive being at an age when you're trying so hard to look cool.

In my third year of high school, even my male classmates had a handy mirror in their pockets. At all times. They would wet their lips, comb their hair and check their looks every other minute. You'd think a ship spilled oil on their heads with the amount of grease they put on their hair to achieve the New Wave look. Didn't matter if a teacher

---

22 Synonyms: boilzit, zitcess.

was giving a lecture, they would always be looking at their faces in the mirror.

One time something got in my eye and I borrowed a mirror from a seatmate to check. That one time was unfortunately also the one time my geometry teacher decided she had enough: "I am telling you; I am going to break that mirror!" I learned later that day that the entire class had a bellyache from holding in their laughter. Everybody agreed that my timing sucked.

High schoolers are notorious when it comes to teasing. I once had a classmate who was dubbed Putok[23] because of his body odor. He was nice, and smart, but every time he was called for recitation, you'd hear our classmates croaking in soft voices: "Poo-tok . . . Poo-tok . . . Poo-tok . . ."

In the same vein, the joke "You and _____ are perfect for each other," which matches you with the unanimously decided ugliest member of the class, was also popular. An unfortunate girl in my freshman year who was almost always mentioned in this joke came to be known as the "beast fighter." I will leave her looks to your imagination.

Just like the heartthrobs and the campus crushes, however, beast fighters do also get written into the history and Who's Who of each graduating class. They, too, get to have their names immortalized along with the wisdom gained from the three most important lessons of the time: the comb, the mirror and the deodorant.

---

23 Stink bomb. *Putok*, literally eruption or explosion, is a vulgar Filipino expression used to describe an unpleasant body odor.

MAKE NO MISTAKE, no class is immune from being un-cool. Like that day when our class of losers had to go round picking up their notebooks scattered in front of the high-school building. How did they get there? Our teacher in Filipino class threw them out the third-floor window.

It was our quarterly submission of notebooks, when our teacher would check if we had completed our chapter summaries of *Noli Me Tangere*.[24] A lot crammed to com-plete their notes, writing their summaries on the spot.

Our teacher started to count as a warning. It was time to leave our work on her desk, which the entire class did. All notebooks were submitted, though some were empty and a lot were incomplete. Whatever, we thought.

"These will be all the notebooks I am going to accept," our teacher said with finality right before she excused her-self and left the room.

In about five seconds, chaos ensued. Everyone charged to the teacher's desk so that they could retrieve their notebooks and add more notes. The place was in uproar. Worse than a Gremlin pool party.

---

24 Classic and important Filipino novel written by the national hero, Jose Rizal; required reading in third year of high school (ninth grade) at the time.

Our teacher came back in a matter of minutes. Because there was a lookout, we managed to put all the notebooks back on her desk in time.

"This just got taller. Why?" she said, irritatingly noticing the difference in the pile. "Who added a notebook here?"

The entire class was apprehensive. As every student was out for his or herself, we wouldn't have known if somebody had added to the pile, or who. And even if we'd known, it was already too late. There was nothing more we could do. We were all in it together.

"I will count to three. Nobody's confessing?" She really was in a bad mood; we suspected perhaps a delayed salary. "One . . . two . . ."

Nobody was owning up to anything. All were holding their breath.

"Three!"

And just like that, our teacher carried all the notebooks to the window and flung them out like confetti on a national holiday parade.

That was our class in Filipino 3. The time I learned about *Noli Me Tangere* and was introduced to Padre Damaso.[25]

---

25 An antagonist priest in the novel.

DRAWING INSPIRATION FROM Jose Rizal's novel after learning about the oppression of the Filipinos by the Spaniards and the courage of Ibarra the protagonist, I once dared to stand up to my teacher in a public speaking and debate class.

This disdainful teacher took pride in his mastery of history and literature, and was a good speaker and philosopher. Which is another way of saying he was a real smart-ass. He'd wind you up in discussions and once you got dizzy, he'd kick you while you were down. He liked quoting passages from different books including the Bible, and he spoke as if William Shakespeare was his lunch buddy. So, I had no idea why I suddenly thought of challenging him that one time. Probably because I couldn't stand him quoting holy verses anymore in the middle of his lecture, I asked where he got them.

"Sir, in which book of the Bible can we see those verses?" The entire class fell silent.

"I'm sorry?" The teacher fell silent.

"In which book of the Bible can we see those verses?"

I tried to stop myself. But by now, everyone in the room was aware that I was embarking on a suicide mission. And those who were already prematurely traumatized wanted to beg for my life:

"Forgive him, Sir, for he knows not what he does!"

Nobody knew I could commit such an unforgivable sin in class. Not even me.

But the wily teacher surpasseth all our understanding. Because he didn't know the answer, he pretended to not take me seriously. Goliath merely laughed off the question that made David the most uncool student in school in an instant. My teacher had once again successfully spun the class around and when they got dizzy, I was the one who got kicked. By recess, everyone just had to hand me their "You had it coming!"

That was just the first round, however. And it wasn't long before the rematch took place. Debate was never my cup of tea. No one would describe me as daring or a jerk, or both. But that was how my classmates started to see me because I never fell for my teacher's cheap tricks. Nor did I ever grant him the reaction he was hoping to get from his audience.

He asked us once, one by one, if we were in favor of divorce. When my turn came, I said no, and quoted from the Bible: "What God hath joined together, let not man put asunder."

"Don't you mind if your spouse is making a fool of you?" he asked sarcastically, as if talking to Forrest Gump.

"No, Sir. I stand by the word of God, Sir." I answered, like Forrest Gump.

I had no arguments that day, I simply wanted to go against any view of my nemesis. As expected, he laughed like a cartoon villain and I just stared at him stoically. This was us for the months that followed. Until we got tired eventually. Because he no longer made fun of the class, I

70

began to respect him. Because I took his subject seriously and no longer challenged him, he began to appreciate me.

I was finally able to see my teacher in Public Speaking and Debate eye to eye. Perhaps that was the lesson on "eloquence" he wanted to deliver. I learned a lot.

HOMILY. Or something like that.

We had a poster and slogan-making contest. It was open to everyone who wanted to take part, including the ones who didn't—that was us, the junior practical arts students.

Practical Arts 3 was tough because the workload was heavy and there was always a project due for submission. I don't think there was anything we hadn't done using pencil, eraser, T-square, drawing board, triangle, foot rule, compass, protractor, pastels, tracing paper, illustration board, construction paper and time.

As always, our class was cramming for our individual contest entries, especially me, and I'd already wasted many days on the "planning stage." I had a good slogan for the anti-drug abuse campaign, which complemented the equally impressive pencil outline on my poster. I was on the right track, except that it was all I had. If I were building a house, all I had was the framework. And the deadline was sixty minutes away.

No problemo, I told myself. A lot of things can happen in two minutes in basketball, so sixty minutes should be enough for my work.

Sadly, I was right. Things did happen in two minutes. A messenger suddenly appeared just outside our door, asking everyone to leave the room and proceed to the lobby for our class' turn to say the rosary. It was October, month of the holy rosary in the Catholic calendar, and at this time every year my nonsectarian school was transfigured into Lourdes.

No one made a sound, but you could hear everybody's single thought: "Holy @&#%$! What happens to my project now?"

And just like that, our teacher asked everyone to leave the room.

"Sir, what about non-Catholics?" said someone, quick to try their luck.

Ingenious. That was a masterstroke. You can never underestimate the mind of a student in dire need. Of course, not all of us are Catholics. And not all of us are Catholics all of the time. Many of us can be Baptists, Buddhists or atheists whenever necessary. And if you're not Catholic, you can stay in the room to work on your project. Hmmm . . . amazing grace!

It was a crucial moment of salvation and a few even became Hindu converts. I myself reconsidered my beliefs when I figured out that it could save my poster. On some level though, I realized it wasn't worth compromising my faith, so I left the room.

Thankfully the rosary didn't take long. We were back in the classroom in no time and were able to catch up with our work. Although still uncolored upon submission, my project received a generous 82% rating. I thought that was good enough while I awaited my beatification.

COOKING WAS ONE OF THE LESSONS in practical arts in my freshman year. It is, after all, a very important life skill. And one of the requirements in class was to prepare a dish, any dish, to be graded by the teacher. My groupmates and I decided we would go for *menudo*, a traditional stew made with pork and sliced liver in tomato sauce with carrots, potatoes and maybe raisins for extra flavor. Not rocket science, but more sophisticated than instant noodle soup which we were sure some other group would settle for.

After consulting with my mother for the recipe, I delegated tasks and asked each member to bring one ingredient—and that included the member who had his Walkman on during the meeting. Everything went well, except on the day we were scheduled to present our dish, because my music-loving groupmate whom I instructed to bring raisins brought potatoes instead,[26] which resulted in a potato-jacked-up version of menudo. Luckily the other group that day did opt for an instant noodle soup, as predicted, and simply submitted their leftovers for the teacher to taste and evaluate, which resulted in us being favored and getting a better grade.

---

26 The word for potatoes is *patatas* in Filipino, while raisins is *pasas*; can be very confusing for anyone who can't be bothered to take their headphones off during a meeting.

Mission accomplished?

Not really. Because we had the same activity in our second year. Menudo's curse.

This time around, our teacher was an elegant woman and we did our cooking in the home economics room where some members of the faculty had their lunch. Our teacher was known as a gracious host and meeting her standards was just another pressure we didn't need.

We were just prepping up when she checked on us and asked if we were cooking anything special.

"Yes, Ma'am . . . we're preparing Mechado!"[27] We'd convinced ourselves that we knew what we were doing. She nodded and left. Only to return and ask if we already had all the ingredients for Afritada.[28]

"Huh?" said my groupmate in a whisper. "Did she say Afritada?"

"Um, Ma'am," I said, trying to clear it up. "We're making Mechado."

Once again, she nodded, left and came back a few moments later to check if our "Afritada" was already done.

"Not yet, Ma'am," I answered, now a bit annoyed. But my groupmate could no longer bear it.

"Ma'am . . . we're cooking Mechado."

The old woman smiled like she hadn't heard anything and went back to her class. My groupmates started to doubt our dish and skill, confused as to what we were really doing.

"As far as I know, this is Mechado!" I said. Soon after, the other teachers started coming in for lunch one by one.

---

27 Beef stew.
28 Chicken, pork or beef stewed in tomato sauce.

"So, what have our students prepared for us today?"

"Afritada!" Our teacher beamed with pride.

Although the combined cooking experience of everyone in the group was limited to hot dogs, omelets and instant noodles, we took offense at the fact that our Mechado was being mistaken for Afritada. Because it just wasn't.

Soon everybody was seated and we served our dish. My group's plates were already filled with food and we were about to eat when we noticed that the teachers had their eyes closed in prayer. And just when we did the same, they started helping themselves to our dish. That was when another teacher entered the room and asked what the good-smelling food was. Everyone at the table replied at the same time with two different answers, leaving the newly arrived teacher perplexed.

Update: I reconnected via social media with the classmate who brought potatoes instead of raisins for our cooking project. He is now busy working as a chef on a luxury cruise ship. Well played, Potato Master! Well played.

MY MOTHER HAD SOME TALENT in making *parol* lanterns,[29] a task usually assigned as a school project during Christmas season. My output was decent because of her. And that was probably the reason I thought of taking part in a lantern-making contest in sophomore year.

I bought a Styrofoam sphere about the size of a basketball to serve as a globe. I already had a cool theme in mind that I wanted to execute: "A World Wrapped in Love at Christmastime." It was a challenging process that would have been more fun if only I wasn't doing it on the night before submission deadline, and my lantern was still unrecognizable. My mother stepped in to do her thing.

Since it was almost one o'clock in the morning, however, and "A World Wrapped in Love at Christmastime" was still not taking shape, my mother called it quits and suggested I buy a lantern on the street instead to donate to school, which was a sound solution since it was allowed by the school in consideration of students' busy schedules before Christmas break. But this, of course, meant ineligibility for the contest, and I was not about to give up the award I knew was reserved for my "World Wrapped in Love at Christmastime." Quitters never win. So, I persevered with my work on this masterpiece, never mind that my mother had already

---

29 Traditional Christmas lanterns, commonly star-shaped.

given up to get some sleep and had left money on the table for a ready-made parol in case I changed my mind. I didn't go to sleep until past two in the morning and was so spent, I failed to get up early for *Simbang Gabi* Mass.[30]

I arrived in school hours later with everyone staring at the impressive lantern I was managing to carry. An elegant big white parol. My teacher asked right away how much I paid for it.

"Thirty-five pesos, Ma'am."

"Child, you've been ripped off. Vendors just outside the gate could give it to you for only thirty pesos."

So, what happened to my "World Wrapped in Love at Christmastime"? I abandoned the struggle and left it lying around until it collected dust under the sofa. It even caught fire once and almost caused serious damage—good thing a bucket of water quickly put it out. The unfortunate globe was mutilated. My "World Wrapped in Love at Christmastime" ended up as "World Whacked by an Asteroid."

---

30 Nine-day series of dawn Masses leading to Christmas Eve.

I MAY BE DEVOID OF TALENT, but I still managed to take part in some school presentations. One of these was a puppet show of Rumpelstiltskin where, other than my trembling hand inside a puppet, no other part of my body performed on stage. It was also unfortunate that our teacher had to recite the beginning of the story using a microphone since the first part of the recorded narration on our cassette tape accidentally got erased.

But that wasn't my one regrettably unforgettable experience on stage. Events were way more tragic in our class production of *Star Wars* for Foundation Day. That's right, *Star Wars*. The girls would make weird dance movements I'd never seen to the movie's iconic theme music and the boys would play galactic warriors I didn't recognize from the movie. Some would be doing ballet, some would be in a battle with explosions and flashing lights. Needless to say, some would also have to make excuses to become a member of a four-man props department instead and be spared from all the indignity of the performance. That would be me.

The show would be performed on an outdoor stage in the school quadrangle. The plan was to prepare black powder on both sides of the stage for a series of sparks and "explosions" that would be ignited with an ember from a mosquito coil attached to the thin branch of a tree. The mosquito coil was for a long-lasting ember, while the branch was for safety—so we wouldn't have to be near the black powder to set it off. My classmate, our team's MacGyver-wannabe leader, had it all figured out.

We lit the mosquito coil at the start of the program to get that first step out of the way. Not unexpectedly, everyone who noticed raised an eyebrow and wondered if we were bothered by mosquitoes. An hour passed and soon all the previous acts were done with their song, dance, poem or acrobatics on stage. It was our turn.

We were all set, except one of our two backdrops—six-by-six-foot (1.8 x 1.8-meter) posters we'd painstakingly taken three days to spray-paint black and silver to achieve the look of outer space—kept falling off the wall. By the time the problem was finally solved, the class was already positioned on stage. The initial reaction we received from the audience was a mix of excitement, curiosity and sarcasm. Somehow none of us was surprised. But anyway—showtime!

The dance had started. It was nearly time for our explosion, but the mosquito coil had almost burned out. We considered running to a nearby grocery store to buy more, but we knew we wouldn't make it in time and the principal would probably be already delivering the program's closing remarks by the time we returned. There was no other choice but to get up on the stage and manually light up our pyrotechnics. Or so we thought. Because our team leader, as always, had a brilliant idea. We would set off our explosions using whatever embers were left on our mosquito coils—plus lots of prayers. But miracle of miracles, it did work! But the double explosion that was supposed to occur on both sides of the stage didn't go off at the same time. The one on the right made a good amount of smoke, and the one on the left followed thirty seconds later with a cute little *pufft*.

The day conspired against us. Even the strobe lights we worked hard to set up didn't help our cause. Because it was only six in the evening and we were outdoors, our inter-galactic lighting was barely noticeable. In hindsight, eating live animals on stage would probably have made our performance a bit more entertaining.

Our teacher didn't say a thing about the show the following day. The class was quiet. Nobody talked about what happened. As if everyone was fresh from a hypnosis session that erased their most recent memory. I am now the only person to admit that such an event took place in our school. And I know my teacher together with my classmates are out to silence me. If anything should happen, you already know my story.

THE LIST OF "TOP TEN STUDENTS" every grading period is based on teachers' standards. It's an elite group established by a class adviser as determined by the students' academic standing, aimed at rewarding diligence with recognition.

Election of the class officers, on the other hand, is based on standards set by the students themselves. The class election is a show of confidence in the classmates they believe are capable of holding big responsibilities and representing them and their interests. Each class is has its own little government. And since my grades were far from perfect, it was in this second group that I got to belong once in a while.

I can longer recall the details, but I do remember getting elected as Sergeant-at-Arms in fourth grade, which means that I was officially entrusted with the task of shouting "Quiet!" in class and telling on everyone to the teacher if yelling wasn't enough. But I didn't get to use these powers because we also had a Discipline Committee with the same function. And they didn't get to use their powers either because our classroom government eventually spiraled into a regime where all dissidents in class only had to buy *yema*[31]

---

31 Sweet custard confectionery made with egg yolks, milk and sugar.

from our teacher[32] to clear their records. Clearly a corrupt system. And fattening.

On account of their incompetence, our two duly elected Sergeant-at-Arms in sixth grade were relieved of their duties by our class adviser, creating a void that called for an appointee deemed worthy of the position.

I was chosen. And not a few flies entered the open mouths of my classmates, who were just as dumbfounded as I was. I had no idea what our teacher had read in her horoscope that day to make such a peculiar move. But I can claim with pride that I was a very effective dictator as called for by the circumstances. Not only did I single-handedly restore and maintain order, I also caused many to cry and made lots of enemies in record time. Most of my classmates made voodoo dolls that they named Roberto Ong with the middle name "I hope you die." And many of them are still in therapy to this day. But I did make one person very happy. Our teacher. Had I been a household product, she would've made a very convincing home TV shopping testimonial for me. Eventually even my classmates learned to appreciate my efforts when they saw the good things brought forth by the new system. So, everybody gave me a hug and surprised me on our graduation day with an award recognizing my valuable contribution in the classroom, just like a Hollywood happy ending. Just kidding. It's a fantasy I still have to this day because nobody at all was pleased with the things I did. And the only reason my life was spared was because the amount of fines collected from every violation resulted in a

---

32 It used to be acceptable for teachers to sell sweets in class to augment their income.

Christmas party with free food and no contribution needed. I did say I was effective.

The moral of the story is that it's not always a bad thing to have enemies because sometimes it means you stood up for something, sometime in your life. Or something like that. It's a quote from Winston Churchill and I don't know much about the guy except that if he were my classmate, I bet he'd be hating on me, too.

SOME SAY THE TIME a Filipino starts becoming a politician is once they join *Kabataang Barangay* (Village Youth) or *Sangguniang Kabataan* (the Youth Council).[33] But that's not true. It all starts in school.

I was in second year of high school when I unintentionally snatched an office from the popular students on campus. There was an election for the sophomore assembly and the first few names nominated belonged to the same familiar faces. Seeing victory was at hand, as always, they all relied on the same hackneyed campaign promises which prompted my bored seatmate to do the craziest thing: nominate me. Our class adviser was, of course, supportive . . . and so were the popular candidates, knowing that I was nominated merely as a laughing stock. When my turn came to deliver a speech, which I didn't have, I resorted to the easiest way out—being honest and funny.

"I will not make any promises . . . because promises are meant to be broken." It was a quote I heard somewhere and it felt right to say it since I really had nothing to say. When your candidacy is a joke and you have nothing to lose, you can say anything and get away with it. Except mine was confoundingly followed with cheers and applause from everyone

---

33 Government-sponsored local youth development councils.

in the room right after a short wave of laughter. I got elected. As most political jokes do.

Two years later, I received another nomination for the General Assembly of the English Club. Once again but with little fanfare this time, I got elected. But that wasn't the highlight of the story. It was the small freshman girl about the size of Smurfette who told another freshman voting for me to put down his hand and "Vote wisely!" A classic snooty move taken from a kid villain in a nineties family movie. When I won, I returned her disdain by dancing in front of her like a raving-mad frilled lizard.[34]

✐ 🖅 ✎

It was in second year of high school that I witnessed the unlikely resignation of our class president. It was unprecedented. I couldn't have imagined anyone doing it. I didn't even know it was possible. She was a smart and capable student, but she left her position in tears, admitting she just couldn't handle the class anymore.

I recently chanced upon a documentary on TV about the possibility of humanity's mass evacuation to another planet in the case of an apocalyptic event. Other than the limitations of technology, one major issue in this scenario would be the establishment of government. What would be the universal currency? Would we still use money? What language would be used? Would everyone have to learn English? Whose beliefs and religions would prevail? How about the system of education or the economy or politics?

---

34 Parts of this story may have only happened in my mind.

What kind of organization would be put in place? And most importantly, who would take the lead and have the final word on every important decision?

Government is a very complex issue and leadership is a massive responsibility. Looking at standard brochures of educational institutions and course outline activities, leadership is often included in the skills taught to students. Looking at the people in power, however, it seems necessary to re-examine whether the teachings on leadership we learned in school are true, right and adequate. Judging by our ability to choose trustworthy people to represent us, it seems we still have so much more to learn about this important aspect of living.

Smurfette has a point. Vote wisely.

FILIPINOS KNOW THE FAMOUS COMEDIANS Salvador Tampac, Pablito Sarmiento and Alfonso Tagle by their popular names: Cachupoy, Babalu and Panchito. But they wouldn't recognize McDo, Bungo (meaning "Skull"), Guchiriz and Baby Tsina ("Baby China"), because these are the cheeky nicknames we used for our teachers behind their backs.

McDo was our underweight and overemotional teacher. She had always considered herself cute, but her long and dangerously pointed chin reminded everyone of the singing quarter moon in a McDonald's commercial.

Bungo was our music teacher, the mastermind of the infamous *Star Wars* production. He wouldn't be called "Skull" if his skull wasn't so obvious beneath his skin. But it didn't matter that he had an X-ray face; he played the piano like a virtuoso and some girls did find him attractive.

Guchiriz's real name was Gutierrez, and she was all right and all good, but her heavy southern Philippines accent was pretty distracting and that earned her this tag. Nevertheless, she could never be more distracting than Baby Tsina who still dressed in the traditional Chinese clothing she wore at the Chinese school where she previously worked.

I wasn't the one who came up with the teachers' nicknames. I don't know how they got their labels and why not all of them had one. Not everyone tagged was a "terror" teacher and not all terror teachers were tagged. The teacher who threw our notebooks out the window was big and heavy, but I don't remember anyone calling her a pig, hippopotamus, dinosaur or Godzilla. Probably because she made it clear from day one that nobody could give her a nickname. And the students complied without question. I admired teachers who commanded such respect.

Still, there were those teachers who didn't need a funny name to be interesting. Just like my physics teacher who was known for announcing her retirement every year but still went on to teach about friction, momentum and potential energy for about twenty more years after I left. It really was all just potential energy, I guess.

My theology professor in college always seemed to lack energy. She was heavy-eyed like Garfield; one would suspect she was always up at night. She would say things like "I am very happy and thankful that all of you supported our outreach programs," but if you didn't listen to what she said and just stared at her face, you'd think the message was: "Our house burned down, my daughter was abused, my husband lost his job and I have cancer."

I also had a science teacher who looked like a firefly with her fondness for clothes, fans and hair colors that were always shimmery. But she was no way a match for the mysterious member of the school staff who always attended the first-Friday Masses at the gym. When her dress was red, so were her shoes, stockings, bag, fan, handkerchief, umbrella and eyeglasses. Everything always matched. Sometimes green, sometimes blue, sometimes yellow. I wouldn't be surprised if she even had a glow-in-the-dark outfit.

I WOKE UP ONE CHRISTMAS to find a toy robot under the Christmas tree. It wasn't gift wrapped. I looked at my parents who were having breakfast.

"Whose is this?" I asked.

"Yours," came an almost impassive answer.

They obviously hadn't taken my question seriously, so I just ignored them. But a few days had passed and the toy was still there. I asked my father again.

"Whose is this really?"

Same vague answer: mine. It was for me. And he went on to remind me of the robot that I had always wanted but couldn't find in all the stores we went to around the city way back when I was nine years old. I could not forget the frustration because there was no worse feeling for a child than to anticipate finally buying his dream toy but going home without it.

"But I'm fifteen years old now!"

I was puzzled. The toy wasn't Transformers. It wasn't Voltron. It wasn't even Voltes V. It was just a one-foot (30-cm)-high low-tech toy that could only be appreciated by a child in grade school. It was a generic robot that walked, made sounds, lit up and had mechanical missiles on its head.

My father was done answering questions. Days passed by and the toy was still under the tree. Neither of my parents gave the toy as a present to another child. They weren't kidding. It really was for me.

I couldn't fool myself into playing with a toy that I no longer wanted. But I kept it as a souvenir and a testament of my father's loyalty in giving me the thing I wanted the most in the world. Didn't matter that it was one childhood too late.

✐ ✏ ✎

I wasn't the type of kid who puts stickers on any old surface in the house or scribbles notes on encyclopedia pages or tears out pages of books and magazines. It was an important rule in our house to take care of and respect our belongings. So, when an activity in fourth year of high school required us to cut out a picture of us and our parents, I simply used photos that were lying around of my father's co-workers abroad and made them my "parents." Friends at school who knew my mother and father smirked, knowing I was pulling off another crazy stunt. Although all I really wanted was to not waste a good photo of my parents for a silly assignment. It was just another disposable homework task, after all, not a school project or anything that would affect my score or class standing.

Sadly, my own parents weren't pleased when they discovered my other "parents." My mother felt sad thinking I was ashamed of them, which was a what-the-heck moment for a teenager who had a very different take on the situation. As baffling as the robot Christmas present was, I couldn't understand why they couldn't appreciate my intention to preserve their photographs. And just as the robot Christmas present took me a long time to understand, it took me a while to realize that what I did had disappointed my mother. And I never felt more sorry.

I am blaming this on inexperience. If I could have another chance at the detestable homework today, I would reprint our entire family album and submit it with a dedication to my teacher: "Here you go, Ma'am. Have a blast!"

SOMETIMES I FEEL BAD when I realize that the only reason I failed to bag an award in high school was my tardiness. It was because I was often late for class that some teachers objected when I was considered for a special award for good conduct—insider info shared by our class adviser to inspire me to do better in college. In hindsight, I probably shouldn't have believed it because I knew that in addition to my problem with punctuality, I had other unreported offenses.

Due to the intense pressure the final exam had on us graduating students, I, together with another wise and wily classmate came up with a scheme. Since the test papers for different subjects were distributed at the same time, we were able to exchange papers and split up the questions, with each one of us answering two papers for each subject. He took care of advanced algebra, trigonometry and physics. I took over world history and literature.

Regrettably, that wasn't the only time I had been dishonest. I also used a cheat sheet written at the back of my Logarithmic Table during an exam. I was even caught. But other than making me feel bad about it, the proctor didn't really do anything else.

All right, I might as well confess everything now.

- I copied my mother's signature to make it appear that I did my English homework at home.

- I wrote my name several times on the chemistry lab countertop (but I swear the letters were no bigger than the text in this book)
- I brought home a book that was just lying around in our classroom (nobody was claiming ownership and since it was battered and dog-eared, chances were it would have ended up in the trash can)
- I often cut classes in some subjects (but not just to hang out, but to finish requirements for other subjects)
- At least half of the reasons used in my excuse letters were mere hallucinations
- I failed to comply with the prescribed haircut and the discipline committee punished me with their own botched version of a haircut
- I broke the uniform rules by wearing a colored under-shirt and was made to stay behind, along with other boys, by the same committee
- The first period teacher caught me sneaking into the gym, along with two of my classmates, while running away from the discipline committee and CAT[35] officers who round up students that are late for flag ceremony
- I was made to pick up trash in the school grounds as punishment many times, along with the other habitual latecomers

To sum up, I violated the rules of attendance and punctuality and haircut and uniform. I was also guilty of charges of

---

35 Citizen Army Training, mandatory military education and training for fourth-year (tenth-grade) high-school students at the time.

cheating, forgery, vandalism and "theft." I apparently had my share of misdeeds, but this went unnoticed because the eyes of school officials were only focused on their usual suspects. Had I been honored with a special award for good conduct, the medal would have only rusted and disintegrated early because I was unworthy. Regardless, my Certificate of Good Moral Character[36] still stated EXEMPLARY.

My reputation was squeaky clean, but not my character. I smelled of politician.

---

36 Standard certification to prove you didn't kill anyone in class or burn the school to the ground; a document usually required for admission to college.

Bob, you're just starting your life. What you've accomplished is but a beginning. I know you've got what it takes to make your life in the future the best. Push hard and you'll be able to achieve what you want with flying colors. I know you could. Congrats and good luck . . .

Lovelots, Ma'am Babes.

LOVELOTS . . . LOVELOTS . . . BABES . . . you won't be able to tell from this how terrifying our class adviser was. She was actually nice, but for most of the students, she was one of the teachers to steer clear of. She was threatening and condescending. Quite the opposite of whoever signed that dedication on my class picture.

We each had our own souvenir ideas come graduation. I had my classmates sign my black school bag using a silver marker. It was so New Wave! This bag now stores my school keepsakes. It's turned into a time capsule containing various artifacts:

- My high-school entrance-fee receipt
- The rental receipt of my graduation toga (with the size indicated)
- Registration cards from first to fourth year of high school

- Report cards from first to fourth year of high school
- My NCEE[37] score report and Certificate of Good Moral Character
- Quiz notebooks (we didn't use loose sheets of paper for quizzes)
- Test papers (some with perfect scores, some flunked)
- Practice tests and examination form for the NCEE
- One pair of black socks
- Bull cap, T-shirt, buckle, tickler (small notebook) and white handkerchief for Citizen Army Training (CAT)
- Student handbook
- Copy of the Teacher Evaluation Form (where we get to strike back at our teachers)
- An excuse letter (composed of made-up excuses)
- Five sheets of white, lined paper repetitively inscribed with "I promise to wear my PE uniform every meeting" (almost everyone in class had to accomplish this)
- Copy of the Opening Remarks I had to deliver in one of our school programs
- Copy of the souvenir programs for our Junior-Senior prom, career orientation lecture and CAT graduation
- My name tag for the class recollection day/retreat
- One long chicken feather, given to me by my classmate during our last CAT classroom instruction, which he found on the school grounds (yes, we had chickens in our school) and told me was the quill pen of Jose Rizal, the author of the greatest Filipino novel, *Noli Me Tangere*

---

37 National College Entrance Exam, similar to the SAT in the US, now abolished.

- A leather wallet, a Christmas gift from a classmate containing the empty wrapper of the Halls candy I chewed during the CAT graduation and the pain reliever pill a "special someone" gave me that day I had a headache in school
- Junior–Senior Prom candle (we failed to light it, due to the strong winds that day)
- Graduation day pictures
- The love letter a "special someone" gave me on our graduation day

TOGETHER WITH MY dorky yet down-to-earth class-mates, we explored colleges in Manila that we might apply for. Revenge of the Nerds, Filipino version.

First stop: University of the East. We marched straight onto the campus, but the security guard stopped us. They were not yet open for applications. "Come back on February 12!" he told us. Disappointed, we went out of the gate. We were already far away when we realized it was February 12 that day.

Second stop: Polytechnic University of the Philippines, PUP, also known as Philippine University of the Philippines. The place immediately gave off a negative vibe. Perhaps because the security guard at the gate was badgering us to buy the self-addressed stamped envelope needed to get the result of the entrance exam or maybe it was their confusing procedures, or the school staff, who were very unaccommodating. We backed out.

Third stop: Centro Escolar University. Seemed OK. On my application form, I wrote "Marketing" as my preferred course. In reality, I hadn't really decided what course to take. I eeny-meeny-miney-moe'd the list just to give an answer.

Fourth stop: Pamantasan ng Lungsod ng Maynila (PLM, College of the City of Manila). I wrote "Computer Science" on my application form, despite having almost zero interest in computers.

Fifth stop: Lyceum of the Philippines. I wasn't able to take the entrance exam with my friends and had to get a new exam date. It was fun though because we were welcomed by students marching in protest.

By God's grace, I passed all the entrance exams, including the one for PLM, where some of the smart guys I know didn't make the grade.

By this time, we'd burned off ten pounds each, gotten lost and suffered from dehydration after walking for so long under the scorching heat of the sun, but I still hadn't found "my school." I knew I needed to go to one more school. Just one more!

I finally found her, after a few more days. It was love at first sight. I may have been thirty minutes late for the exam, but it still turned out well. Some say I was lucky that I was still allowed to take the test despite my tardiness: they didn't usually tolerate that. I was about to write "Computer Science" for my subject choice, but the office assistant told me they didn't have that course. I went for the next computer course on the list. As long as there was "computer" in the name, I was fine with that.

Finally, I was at college! I could hear the Voltes V theme song playing in my head.

BUT I HAVE NO OTHER COLLEGE STORIES to share. The end.

I can hardly remember any stories at all. Maybe it's because I tried to wipe out all my memories the day I burned all my belongings.

I sometimes think I died at seventeen years old, despite not being put below the ground.

My first experience with outright rejection came on my seventeenth birthday. It was the morning of my first quarter exams and the traffic was horrendous. I arrived late for my first class. My economics professor refused to let me take it. Instead, he instructed me to go the Dean's office to apply for a special exam, which I would have to take alongside students from another class. So, I proceeded to the Dean's office. When I arrived, I was told that my economics professor was justified in not letting me take the exam and that I had no acceptable reason for being late. So . . . no special test.

I tried to explain. I said that the instructor didn't really "not allow" me to take the test. He simply thought I wouldn't be able to finish the test in time, so he suggested I take it with students from a different class.

"I'm sorry, I don't see any reason at all to grant you a special permit," the Dean's assistant said. After bargaining some more, I realized he was right. My argument was illogical, even to myself. I had made a blunder; I don't exactly know what compelled me to let my economics professor throw me out of the exam. I had made it to the exam room, albeit late. Why didn't he just let me take the exam? Also, if he was even remotely concerned about me, why did he require me to get a special permit? After all, it was his idea that I take the test with a different class.

Too bad. Had I been allowed to take the test despite coming late, I could have answered half of the questions at least. I'd like to think I have common sense, but I chose to be stupid. I admit, my tardiness was my fault. But my worst fault was not standing up for my rights.

I left school in a daze. I was so out of it that I was almost run over by a car. That's when I realized this is what college is all about—dirty tricks.

TEN TRAIN STATIONS, two jeepney rides, fifteen minutes or more of walking and almost a hundred steps of stairs—six times a week. That was just my one-way travel to school during my first semester, not including the time spent going off campus for lunch. Exhaustion, sleepless nights, skipped meals, tons of homework—these were the things that welcomed my frail ninety-five-pound frame at college.

I was often late for class. As soon as I was seated, I would wring out my sweat-soaked handkerchief. Afterward, I'd let the cloth dry over my thigh and then the wetness would seep through my pants. It was fine—they dried soon enough in an air-conditioned room, along with the sweat on my back. As soon as I got home, I'd be out like a light. No time for meals. Whatever time I had left wasn't even enough to start my homework.

Fatigue? Burnout? I don't know. I was stuck in this rut for weeks. I was always chasing time and there never seemed to be enough of it.

I arrived late to class again one day. The instructor refused to accept my science project. I knew what that meant.

First year. First semester. First time. I flunked General Science 101.

My tardiness worsened; my absences hit a peak. That was basically what the second semester was all about. At that point, I still had no idea where I was headed with my studies. I had to retake one class, but no biggie. I was like that actor in an action flick with a grazing bullet wound on his arm—hurt but still standing. One failed subject was nothing. I even managed to cheer up a classmate who flunked just a minor subject.

I still got decent scores in my quizzes and exams. Every now and then, I'd get noticed by my teachers in class. However, my grades hovered around 75% (the lowest mark) because of the missed quizzes, missed recitations, missed projects, missed exams. Misery.

When my finals arrived, I was as sick as a dog. The finals lasted a week and I was absent the entire time. The balls that I had been juggling throughout the semester fell to the ground. I failed six units and had nine others that were incomplete. This time, I wasn't just grazed on the arm by a bullet. I was the ball shot from a cannon.

Retaking a subject was more convenient than having to follow a professor around to complete a requirement.

I enrolled in summer classes.

It was a step in the right direction. I retook one of the subjects I failed right away and decided to take up another class in advance, to maximize my transportation money.

At last! The move paid off and for some time I was able to forget about my recent blunders. Those summer classes were a good experience. I regained both my physical strength and interest in my studies. Perhaps because it was summer break and traffic wasn't too bad on the way to school. Maybe it was because there weren't a lot of students at school. That meant that classes were less chaotic and teachers could concentrate on teaching the lessons. Perhaps it was because my instructors were different. They were more knowledgeable, more diligent and more patient. And they did more than use their finger to point at students during class. They called students by their name. Yes, my instructors that summer actually knew me.

Awesome. My college report card had bragging rights once again.

HOWEVER, IN MY SECOND YEAR, college life went back to its original form—a jungle. I, too, reverted to my old form—an insect. I started to lose all interest in school. I had the one class I'd taken in advance, but many others I needed to retake. My schedule was all jumbled up. I was separated from my friends and had to sit in class with people I didn't know. My free periods were all over the place

I used to skip class once or twice a week, now I was attending class only when I wanted—my absences outnumbered my attendance. It wasn't like I was lazy or anything. Not at all. I'd go about my usual routine each morning. Get up. Have breakfast. Take a shower. Get dressed. And just as I was about ready to leave, I would change my mind and decide that I didn't want to go to class anymore.

My classmates noticed this pattern and tried psyching me up with pep talks. But they eventually grew tired of it.

I had five college units that I had to save this semester.

✐ ✐ ✐

Second year, second semester, second life. I would have been done with college had it not been for my sister, who enrolled me. I had already given up. I wasn't going through enrollment again. I didn't want to know how much more I had to endure to get that blasted diploma.

Accounting 1 was six units. That meant sitting through three-hour classes twice a week. I retook the class three times; I'd gotten to the point of memorizing all the exam questions. Yet, I could never last the semester and always dropped out. Accounting 1 was a prerequisite. There was still Accounting 2 and 3, along with Business Orientation 1, 2 and 3, all of which I had to take at the same time.

Cursed diploma.

✐ ✏ ✎

I took summer classes again thinking it could help resuscitate my interest. Two months of summer studies—I lasted only one. My tank was empty. I'd had enough.

I looked for a new life in a new school. I found one just in time for the start of classes.

The school was fine, as were the faculty, students and life in general. I was able to quickly adjust to my new surroundings. Good for me. Or so I thought.

Finals came and I was sick again. If that wasn't bad enough, I lost my school ID and registration card, which I needed for my exam permit. The night before the exams, I couldn't decide what to do first: finish school projects and reports due for submission? Revise for the tests? Produce a new ID and registration card from thin air so I could get a permit? Or follow my doctor's advice to take it easy and sleep more if I didn't want to wind up in a hospital bed?

The air was cold. Christmas was approaching. It was the middle of the night, so quiet you could hear the fire in your heart dying. I knew very well that whatever decision I made would shape my future. Long term. Lifetime.

I took my meds then went to bed.

I didn't show up for the exam.

BEFORE LONG, CHRISTMAS WAS OVER and I needed to deal with my problems once again. It was only January, yet it felt as if it were Lent. There was no way I was telling my family that I had messed up again. I had bungled up too many times. Far too many. Over and over.

I kept everything under wraps. When school resumed, I pretended I was attending classes even though I wasn't enrolled, even when I had five incomplete subjects that needed saving from purgatory. I continued to leave the house every day, asking for transportation money just like a regular student. But all I did was kill time in Manila, meandering through the city.

THEY SAY THAT NO MATTER THE PROBLEM, the only person who can help you is yourself. They are right. I ended up blowing my own cover.

There was a ruckus one evening during dinner with my siblings and some guests. I started it. It wasn't my intention but it happened anyway. Maybe I wanted to let everyone know what a big mess I was in.

The final straw. That night, I sat down and wrote down everything that I wanted to say. A letter of apology. It's possible that God gave us a conscience because He realized people didn't always use their heads.

It was quite lengthy. I wrote about my struggles at school. I wrote about my simple dreams, fears, joys, anger, grief and regrets. I had cracked under pressure without realizing it. My family was going through some troubles as well, so I hadn't give myself a chance to ask for help.

I wrote in the letter that I wasn't into drugs, or gambling, or any vice at all. I'd just lost interest in school. My mind was muddled. I was exhausted. College just wasn't for me. I'd run out of patience, lost hope and lost my dreams.

I felt like a piece of paper that already had too many erasures on it and just had to be thrown out. I confessed that the idea of using a gun had once crossed my mind. The world wouldn't mourn the loss of one person anyway.

I wrote down what I couldn't personally tell them.

That same night, my eldest sibling talked to me just outside my room to comfort me. Teary-eyed, voice breaking and words trembling, I finally admitted my defeat. At times, it takes bravery to confess our weaknesses. That was the first time I saw my whole family stop to pay attention to their youngest member. I asked them only one thing: to allow me to stumble without being ridiculed, or confronted, or questioned, or reminded about the number of times I failed and needed to try again.

My parents were away that time. My mother was in the provinces; my father was stationed on a ship. It took some time before I was able to speak with them. I was aware of how depressing the news that I had dropped out of college must have been for them. But I also knew what was on my father's mind—the situation was more heartbreaking for me than for anyone else. He asked questions; what happened, what my plans were, but never asked for an explanation. In the short time that we talked, he made me feel I was steering my own ship. It was my job to voyage, to go where I wanted to. My life was my responsibility.

✐ ✐ ✐

I received a call one day from one of my college friends. It had been six months since I left my previous university. I had steered clear of my friends for a long time because I didn't want them to feel bad that I had given up despite their moral support.

They were in a tight spot with their group thesis: none of them had a computer at home. This time, they needed my help. I knew that if they knew someone else who could

120

help them, they wouldn't bother me. That's when it hit me. Despite my misery and severe depression, I could still help others, if only I wasn't too wrapped up in myself.

I swallowed my childish pride and bravely faced them, in spite of my insecurity. The judgment my immature mind had anticipated didn't happen. They were the good kind of friends. I was right to trust and now understood what real friendship was worth.

I could do more if only I didn't limit myself.

THE STORM HAD FINALLY PASSED. When it was over, I was a completely different person. My worldview changed. My opinions evolved and improved. As for what to do with the rest of my life . . . I wasn't too sure about that.

I had no intention of returning to school. I was keen on learning more but I just didn't want to go back. My desire to graduate was merely because I wanted to tell everyone I had a degree—whatever degree it was. My yearning for a diploma was only because I needed something to patch up the hole in my life.

A university degree was a ritual, a tradition, a sacrament, a requirement imposed by society on people who yearn for a place in the workforce and to earn an honest living. And yes, it was something that you needed to gain people's respect.

I did go back to school but I enrolled on a technical course. A two-year computer course. It made me uneasy when people called it a "vocational course," which made it sound so unimportant or when they referred to it as "just a two-year course." Not a college course, nor a university course. It was a "mere" two-year course at a "mere" learning center. It wasn't Computer Science or Computer Engineering. It was "merely" Computer Programming.

Just like many others, I used to look down on dropouts and vocational school graduates. Now that I was part of the group, I felt differently.

The demography of the two-year courses was quite different. Most students who enrolled came from public high schools. People had this misconception that vocational school students were dull. The only difference between vocational students and college students was that in vocational school, there was a lower ratio of well-performing students which may be attributed to inequality. No less smart, just fewer achievers.

I SPENT TWO YEARS at the first college I attended, one semester at the college I transferred to and finally another two years in a vocational school. Despite throwing away my pride, admitting defeat and accepting the fact that I ended up studying a "mere" vocational course, I have to say that this new school was nirvana.

It was a modest building. The entire campus was housed on a single floor and had no basketball court, gym, quadrangle, trees, drinking fountain or audio-visual room. The canteen, clinic, library, faculty room and restrooms were compact versions of the ones in universities. Definitely not for the claustrophobic.

But it was in this school that I was able to take a breather. Even if the students were lacking in humor, they didn't annoy you with stories of their fancy cars and lifestyles. The teachers weren't the best but they were always available when students needed them. We didn't have to follow them around like crazed fans of rock stars. Everyone was personable, accommodating and easy to chat with.

But the battle was far from over.

I had to convince myself to not go down the same path to destruction again. I sought for inspiration. This came in the form of a straightforward school newsletter. In two years, I started at the bottom as a contributing writer and worked my way up to become editor-in-chief. With the help of my co-editors who came from different colleges and carried their own problematic pasts, we got extra funding for the paper which flourished after major improvements and was recognized as an official publication for the first time.

Our young organization was far from perfect. But me and my colleagues were able to make headway, build a bridge and establish a system. That was our achievement.

It was also a reason to remain in school. Instead of skipping class like I used to, I found myself attending meetings and staying until the school closed for the day. The administration was so impressed with the organization, we were entrusted with a few other responsibilities beyond our scope.

I was finally able to finish school. But I didn't attend the graduation ceremony. While my classmates were marching onto the stage to get their diplomas, I was at another school—teaching.

✐ ✏ ✎

I'd got a job in another school where I taught basic and advanced computer skills to professionals. Apart from the need to sharpen my ax by reading up and learning more so I could master the subject, I also had to work on my English and to upgrade my outfit from the usual shirt and jeans to a more polished buttoned shirt and slacks ensemble. But it was all good. The adjustment was a piece of cake and it benefited me as much as it did my class. This was officially my very first work experience and it turned out to be not so different from going back to school. Any challenge was manageable and I learned to relate to all kinds of people.

Well, not all.

AFTER OVER A YEAR in my profession, the company I worked for, which also provided computer education in elementary and high schools, informed me that they needed to send me to a private school as an emergency substitute teacher. Without a choice, I agreed to the job on the understanding that it would only be for a week or so. But due to a lack of qualified applicants for the immediate position, I was asked to reconsider and accept the assignment for the entire academic year right after the day I said yes. Did I hear it right? It was a bait-and-switch appointment. Steam came out of my ears. I hadn't signed up for a permanent job I was neither interested in nor qualified to do. They were practically asking me to chew glass shards.

I agreed to fill in for a month as a compromise, to give the company more time, because I understood that they were a fledgling organization and really didn't have anybody else available to take on the job. Besides, I'd been treated very well prior to this. So be it then. I was going to teach in high school—the litmus test for teachers—and chew glass shards!

The day of reckoning arrived. I had a briefing with the principal. I was given a teacher's manual, a class record book and a big notebook for lesson planning. I was taught how to compute grades and was given last-minute advice. I scarcely had time to mull things over. I wasn't given the

option to reconsider. I returned home, the sun set and rose. Ting! Fight! I felt as if I had been thrown into a boxing ring. The sun's magnificent rays that morning seemed insulting, greeting me sarcastically, "Good morning, Teacher!"

✐ ✏ ✎

My first day on the job.

This was outrageous! Back in high school, I barely made it to flag-raising ceremony every morning. I was always rushing to get in the line or sometimes just cut classes to avoid the Citizen Army Training officers on lookout for latecomers. And here I was, back in high school and a teacher at that!

I couldn't believe how my feet carried me to the faculty room. Holy cow! This was real. I was a T-E-A-C-H-E-R. Yikes! Wherever I looked, I saw teachers. Everywhere there were chalk boxes, class records, chalk boxes, books, chalk boxes, erasers, chalk boxes, chalk—

"Hi! Good morning!" said another teacher, recruited by the same company. We were a dual force sent to the school.

"Sorry, I don't think I can pretend having good mornings here," I said. We both laughed off our anxiety at this new job.

Someone exclaimed, "Oh, look! We've got some young teachers here!" When we looked around, we saw that all eyes were on us. We returned the other teachers' smiles, although it felt as if we were inmates waiting to be initiated.

The bell rang. We each went our separate ways to our first class. For the true-blue teacher, it was a brand-new day of promoting learning and battling ignorance. For me, it felt like my last day on earth.

"As I walk through the valley of the shadow of death—" The soundtrack of the movie *Dangerous Minds* played in my head as I headed toward the classroom. Because classes had not yet begun on a regular schedule, students were scattered throughout the corridors. My class was on the fourth floor, the top floor of the building. By the time I got to the third floor, I felt the urge to retreat.

After a few more steps, I reached the classroom. I knew I looked polished and respectable. As I took my place in front of the class, a student asked, "Sir, is this your first time teaching?" I said no, I'd taught previously in another school. But jeepers, my defense had been breached! I was obviously a nervous newbie, sweating buckets.

The students bombarded me with questions. I didn't answer. Instead, I asked the students who were still loitering outside to come in. Class was about to start.

"But Sir, it's too early!" quipped a young lady.

"What time does the class start anyway?" I asked. In sudden panic, suspecting something was amiss, I started leafing through my copy of the class schedule without waiting for her reply.

The rest of the students made their way inside the room. Many students continued with their chatter, but most students had already turned their attention to me. My mind was elsewhere. As I looked at my class schedule, I couldn't believe my eyes. I WAS IN THE WRONG ROOM AND THIS WASN'T MY CLASS!

Jumping Jupiter!

What a great start! I pretended not to make a fuss. In a diplomatic tone, I introduced myself. "My name is Roberto Ong. I'm going to be your computer teacher. But right now, there seems to be a problem with your schedule, so I'll have to see Mrs. Santillan first. We'll start next meeting." I made a clean getaway and ran to the other room where my class had been waiting for me for ten minutes already. Whew!

SCUBA DIVERS SAY about the depths of the oceans, "It's a different world down there."

Sky divers say about the skies, "It's a different world up there."

As a high-school teacher, the only thing I can say is this, "It's a different world behind a teacher's desk."

So different. Very, very different. As a student, it's difficult to imagine why noise appears to be toxic to a teacher. As a teacher, it's challenging to think how not making noise could seem life-threatening for a student. Every kind of noise aggravated me, even when I knew a student was merely asking his seatmate for the time, or asking a classmate to move their seat back a bit, or just inviting someone to the canteen after class. Whatever sounds, however faint, made at the same time as I was speaking, irritated me. I could hear everything around me as if I wore a hearing aid or possessed sonar abilities.

It was also challenging to be fair as a teacher, to avoid playing favorites. The intelligent, the diligent, the goody-two-shoes, the teacher's pet that I used to loathe as a student, were angels to me now.

IN THE EYES OF A TEACHER, there are twelve types of high-school student.

Clowns: The official class jesters, who perk up the class with their one-liners. A teacher once told me that these are the attention seekers who compensate for their mediocre IQs by making jokes and being silly. I'm afraid there's one in every class, which makes it even harder for teachers to go to school every day.

Geeks: Oblivious to the world and just concerned about books, teachers and the blackboard. No matter how foul the teacher's mood is, these students never hesitate to approach and ask whether substituting the value of x with y would yield the same result or not.

Hollow Men: The HM virus comes in two forms. Type As are often invisible—their seats usually empty because they never come to class. Type Bs, on the other hand, never miss a class. It's their answers to test questions that are always missing.

Spice Girls: A clique of girls who love to party together and arrive late together after recess and lunch break. They always have combs, brushes and a copy of *Song Hits*[38]

---

38 A popular Filipino magazine in the nineties and earlier.

on hand. Whenever you asked students to form groups, the Spice Girls would always band together.

The Gwapings:[39] Male counterparts of the Spice Girls, who were born with too much confidence. Usually, this group is smaller, with only two to four members, so everyone can get stellar attention. Much like the Spice Girls, all they care about is hair gel.

Celebrities: Politicians, athletes and performers. Politicians are the militant ones who worry more about the welfare of students and the school than their grades in algebra. Athletes are the varsity members who can't read as fast as they can run. Performers are the students who seem to attend school only to sing, dance and recite poems on stage during Language Week. The celebrities are stereotyped as having great PR skills and low IQs.

Guinness Record Holders: These students hold records for being the most persistent. Their tenacity compensates for their lack of intelligence. They often end up being successful in life. They turn in projects on time and participate enthusiastically in class. They frequently raise their hands but also frequently give the wrong answers.

Leather Goods: Students with determination, but the wrong kind. They are determined to cheat and resort to flattery to stay in the good graces of the teacher. Their skin is as thick as an alligator's.

Weirdos: Troubled students who claim to be misunderstood. Often referred to as the black sheep of the

---

39 Named after the popular group of handsome teenage boys on TV.

class. They have a distinct set of traits: a small group of friends, a penchant for fistfights, a lack of interest in school and a hatred of teachers.

Children of Rizal: A school's endangered species. Straight A students, but well rounded and not geeks. Teacher's pets, but not sycophants. They lord over others in math, science and English but still have time for extracurricular activities and fun.

Bob Ongs: Partly intelligent, partly nutty. These are the students who sit out lectures thinking up the next book to publish about their classmates.

Commoners: Generic members of the class. Lack individuality or characteristics that leave an impression. Teachers hardly notice their absence. And as time goes by, they are easily forgotten by teachers and classmates.

It is possible for a student to be a combination of the types mentioned above. It's also possible to not come across all types in one class.

THAT WAS THE FIRST TIME in my entire life that I fell asleep in a jeepney from extreme exhaustion. And, for the first time in a long time, I got back into the dreary routine of turning in early and getting up early. It dawned on me that being a teacher was one tough job.

I struggled with lesson planning every day. It felt like I was a student hitting the books again. Everything I had learned in the past had to be updated. The knowledge I had accumulated over the years still needed to be expanded.

Each of my classes resembled a large family, with me as the head of it. My students' problems were my problems as well. Whatever issues affected their studies affected my classes too.

It was my responsibility to manage the class, to mediate fights, to wake the sleepyheads, to make the shy ones talk, to prod the lazy ones to work and, in some instances, to lend an ear to ease the burdens students carried.

Whenever the class was rowdy, the classroom in disarray or when students underperformed, I was held accountable by the school principal. As teacher I may have been head of a class, but I also worked with a boss and colleagues and had parents that I needed to get along with.

Everything was scrutinized: my appearance, clothing, gestures, words and lifestyle. If by the end of the day, I had managed not to lash out at a hard-headed student, avoided making an error that needed explaining to the Department of Education and successfully balanced my role as a teacher and a colleague, I would earn one thing—respect, which was like a revolving fund that I dipped into to make it through another day as an educator.

I READ A NEWSPAPER STORY about a principal in the USA who ate worms to get students in elementary school to read. It all started when the principal wagered that he would eat a worm for every two books a student read, to support the school's reading initiative. The students began reading and the principal kept his promise.

Though I've never heard of Filipino teachers doing the same, I'm sure there are a lot of hardworking teachers here. Eating worms is unnecessary. Working side jobs to supplement their low income and feed their families three meals a day is proof enough. Traversing mountains and rivers every day to teach first and second graders in a joint class in the middle of nowhere is proof enough. Having to teach while steeped in floodwaters or under a bare tree after a typhoon ravaged the hut that used to be the classroom is proof enough. Putting up with bureaucracy, politics and corruption every day is proof enough. Experiencing sleepless nights, exhaustion, missing meal times on election days,[40] confronting the threat of being kidnapped and beheaded by rebels in far-flung areas, putting up with low wages, delayed wages and no wages for all the extra work done at home are all proof enough. No, eating worms is unnecessary.

---

40 Public school teachers serve as poll workers in classrooms that function as voting precincts during election.

Teachers are the "new breed of heroes" but haven't been given the title because they don't bring in dollars for the country, unlike overseas Filipino workers. The truth is, countless Filipinos are heroes. The problem lies in us being a developing country with three classes of citizens: the poor, the poorer and the rich and powerful opportunists who created the two.

Teaching is one of the lowest-paying professions in the United States, much like in the Philippines. Even the better teaching jobs don't pay enough to make anyone wealthy. Domestic helpers who work in other countries are paid higher; their jobs are easier. If money is what drives you, don't be a teacher. To work as a teacher is difficult. Teaching is a mission, a "vocation" as they say.

I MUST HAVE EXPERIENCED Stockholm Syndrome while behind the teacher's desk, as I developed a higher regard for the teaching profession. To my mind, teaching is the most sacred job in the world. Soon after children take their first steps, they are sent to school and left to the care of teachers. In the Philippines a teacher usually cares for a class of fifty children. That's fifty lives, fifty dreams, fifty "hopes of the nation." The teacher affects who among these fifty will turn out to be a leader of the country, a murderer, a celebrity, the discoverer of the cure for AIDS, an illegal recruiter, a tycoon or another teacher. "A teacher affects eternity," said historian and journalist Henry Adams, "He can never tell where his influence stops."

I wonder how the music teacher of renowned Filipino pianist Lucresia Kasilag, or the PE teacher of World Bowling Hall of Famer Paeng Nepomuceno, or the social studies teacher of statesman and president of the UN General Assembly Carlos Romulo felt. I wonder who Einstein's teacher was, or Shakespeare's, Beethoven's, or Gandhi's. I wonder what it would be like if the person whom the twelve disciples call teacher was my teacher too.

A teacher affects eternity. Plato was a student of Socrates. Aristotle learned from Plato. And Aristotle educated Macedonian king Alexander the Great, who would go on to become one of the greatest military leaders of all time. Who can say that the legacy of Socrates has faded, despite the passage of more than two millennia?

In the Philippines, in June 2003, there was a shortage of 31 million textbooks, of more than 35,000 classrooms and of 90,000 school washrooms. There were no seats in the classroom for 908,000 Alexanders the Great. And students lacked 60,000 Socrates to teach them all. There were often around 60 students per class. There were days when classes were held on Saturdays, in the evenings or early mornings, just to accommodate students.

A 292 billion peso budget. Twenty million basic education students in public schools. One child in every ten between the ages of six and eleven not enrolled in elementary school. Four out of ten children between the ages of twelve and fifteen not in high school. Six out of ten first-grade pupils not finishing a full ten years of education.

According to UNESCO, the Philippines, with 1.5 million children out of school in 2011, falls behind India, which falls behind Ethiopia, Pakistan and Nigeria. The Philippines ranked fifth in the world in the number of children deprived of elementary education.

Department of Education data revealed that the teacher-student ratio was 1:37, which the Teacher's Dignity Coalition insisted was actually 1:45 and sometimes 1:60. Whichever is correct, we aren't far behind Congo, Pakistan and Bangladesh.

As recommended by the United Nations, 6 percent of the country's gross domestic product should be set aside for the population's basic education. However, according to the Human Development Index in 2008, our 2.8 percent allocation ranked us 151st in the world, while Vietnam ranked 61st with 5.3 percent.

A new edition of this book was released to provide timely information about the state of education of the country. However, because I am not a statistician and this book isn't sufficient as a resource, it probably suffices to point out the above facts for us to get a better understanding of how things are in the Philippines now. If the numbers improve in the coming years, then good. If they worsen, it means we didn't employ solutions that were within our grasp. We can't blame books for that.

THESE WERE SOME OF THE THINGS you'd glean from learning materials used in schools, complete with original grammatical errors.

- He cleaned the forests.
- Cemetery is the antonym of pharmacy.
- The woman moved as a distinct population.
- Our people are suffering like no hell on earth.
- Monologue: a continuous series of jokes or comic stories.
- Businesses are more accepting of women performing business.
- Exhibit makes use of effects but occasionally distract the content.
- A dictionary uses the most frequent words in English in their definitions.
- Reading is beyond enjoyable if you don't understand the reading selection.
- You can stop someone dominating the conversation and you can include quieter people.
- Many times the messages you convey are not understood because of the manner you say them, specially so when conversations are carried out in monologues.
- Family members don't hesitate to pursue fields of endeavor that would bring them honor and glory. Take for example the political dynasty we have in the country.

- Filipinos are part of the Asian continent. Filipinos and Thais have water dwellers.

Former Academic Director Antonio Calipjo Go's contribution to education cannot be discounted. It was he who pointed out to the Department of Education the controversial issue of the many errors in textbooks used in schools over the last decade. And because the problem never went away, the discussions and debates continue to this day. But if everything results in textbook reform and a prudent procurement program within the Department—which I hope happens—I believe we and the next generation of Filipinos are bound to benefit greatly.

THE FIRST TIME I heard of the Department of Education, Culture and Sports (DECS) was in grade school when we were given the task of naming all the branches of government and their corresponding secretaries. That and from diligently waiting by the radio for class suspension announcements from the department head every time it rained. The slightest flicker of lightning through the skies would always give me hope. Who knows? They just might call off classes today.

Nowadays, the local government and the DepEd make such announcements, not the DECS. If your age has exceeded the number of days in a calendar month, here's a quick review of other recent educational changes.

1988: Free education was implemented in public high schools. Prior to this, students had to shell out various fees, as well as shelling out for whatever things their teachers sold to them. The peddling continues, and sometimes perpetrators get featured on the evening news bulletins.

1994: The number of school days increased from 185 to 200 to keep students from binge-watching *Ang TV* or the Universal Motion Dancers.[41]

1994: Final year high-school students were directed to take the National Secondary Assessment Test measuring teachers' and schools' so-called honesty (more on this later).

---

41 A popular youth-oriented TV show in the nineties and a popular dance group.

This replaced the National College Entrance Examinations which had hindered college admission for underprivileged students in the boondocks who didn't get the same quality of education but were subjected to a standardized test.

1994: The Commission on Higher Education was established to oversee the Waterproof Students of the Philippines (College students who have to attend school despite typhoons and must wakeboard through floodwaters, unless the government raise a Level 3 typhoon alert.)

1994: Still "on a high" after hosting the Miss Universe pageant, the government established the Technical Education and Skills Development Authority to manage vocational, technical and non-professional courses. (If I have not lost you yet, the changes mentioned here simply lightened the Department of Education's overload of responsibilities, which used to include culture and sports.)

2001: The former Department of Education, Culture and Sports was now named the Department of Education or DepEd. Thalia, K-Pop and anime took care of the culture part, while the boxing icon Pacquiao took care of the sports part.

2002: The National Service Training Program replaced Citizen Army Training in high school, and the mandatory Reserve Officers' Training Corps (ROTC) for male college students became optional and shorter. Aside from the ROTC, students could choose the Literacy Training Service, where they could teach indigent youth or the Civic Welfare Training Service, which fostered civic consciousness.[42]

---

42 Update: The current administration is bringing back mandatory youth military training. Just in time for wars, diseases and despotism coming back into fashion.

IN 2011, THE DEPARTMENT OF EDUCATION adopted a K–12 education system significantly different from the previous system. If a student nowadays wrote their own version of this book, the stories would be quite different.

Children aged five are required to attend kindergarten under the K–12 system. They enter first grade at the age of six. As with the previous system, they complete elementary education in six years. At the age of twelve, they enter junior high school for four years. They enter senior high school at the age of sixteen.

Kindergartners will be taught the same subjects as before the 2011 reform, but instructions will be delivered in their region's local languages: Waray, Iloko, Tagalog or whatever their mother tongue is. First graders can read in their native language. English and Filipino are added to their curriculum as separate subjects. These languages become the medium of instruction beginning in the fourth grade and continuing through senior high school.

Students in junior high school now study various disciplines interconnectedly in a "spiral progression" technique. This means they don't have to wait until high school before they can study subjects such as algebra, geometry, biology, earth science or chemistry.

When students reach senior high school, they are segregated based on their specializations. Aside from the core curriculum of literature, communication, languages, philosophy, mathematics, natural sciences and social sciences, there are various tracks based on students' interests and career goals: Technical-Vocational-Livelihood (TVL); Sports and Arts (SA); and the Academic, which includes Business, Accounting and Management (BAM), Humanities, Education, Social Sciences (HESS); and Science, Technology, Engineering, Mathematics (STEM).

After finishing senior high school, students now have the options to work, start their own business or pursue a college education. Changes in tertiary education are major but not nothing complicated and the new system guarantees students can earn a living after only two years of senior high school or even while studying.

There are many more specifics in the program. Still, I like K–12 because it recognizes children's diversity and draws attention to the fact that not all citizens can, want or should go to college. Are there flaws in the system? Definitely, and many are unhappy. However, because the program is in place, we are forced to confront and address issues that may arise. There will almost certainly be many more changes in the future, making the information in this book obsolete, but for the time being, this is the Philippine education system.

I had a classmate in grade school whom I helped with an essay assignment minutes before the teacher arrived. I wasn't aware that the essay was snatched from him by the class president who hadn't done his homework either. The incident left my classmate in shock, like the bullied kid you'd see in a movie. And it happened at the wrong time since that day, our teacher who was usually pleasant, was in a foul mood. All those without homework were told to stand for the entire period as punishment.

Our class president who cheated and stole an assignment and went on to become a consistent honors student, is now living the good life in another country.

The term "whistleblower" is a recent addition to the Filipino lexicon and consciousness in the past decade. It refers to an individual who exposes an organization's corrupt and illegal activities. I'm not sure whether having more and more whistleblowers coming out lately to expose anomalies in the government is a good thing or if it only shows that there is much more corruption that needs to be brought to light.

There was a particular day at the beginning of this year when I was disheartened by the news of government corruption. The cries of the people protesting about corrupt government officials were deafening. People had had enough of lies. They had grown tired of crooks. But on this same day, I was shortchanged by a dishonest cashier and overcharged by a shameless tricycle driver.

It is easy to understand how "power corrupts." But what if even those who are not yet in power are already thirsty for excess? Is cheating more justified if the person is poorer? Where does such a desire to deceive others come from and what role does education play in resolving it? Or is education to be blamed too?

Is cheating in exams a serious offense? If not, how negligible is it? Is our work ethic in private companies or in the government linked to the honesty or dishonesty that we cultivate in school?

We often get confused with our own concept of education. From our testing method in class intended to highlight parts of lessons that require more attention, the system has evolved into a means of distinguishing students who should be glorified with honors from ordinary students who are often left behind.

There were numerous instances in my public elementary school where teachers blatantly dictated National Achievement Test answers. The school had no choice, they claimed, they need to improve, or at least sustain, its ranking to receive adequate support and funding.

A flawed system. Remedied by an even more messed-up system. That reinforced the roots of an egregious system.

MY SHORT STINT as a high school substitute teacher came to an end in less than a month. I returned to teaching professionals right after, and left the teaching profession entirely after nearly three years. I found it ironic that I was back in school as a teacher when I'd avoided school as a student. I knew I wasn't so bad and I must admit I enjoyed it somehow—but I also knew in my heart it wasn't my destiny to teach. At least not as a school teacher.

Teaching is a vocation. Perhaps that is why some who pursued courses in teaching didn't go on to become teachers and some who did end up as educators were those who never really dreamed of teaching.

I didn't want to be a teacher because I disliked studying. And to go on teaching meant going back to school for the necessary credentials. But I refused to go back to school, either as a teacher or as a student. Anyone who attempted to talk me out of it then was asking for trouble.

OUR HIGH SCHOOL REUNION was coming up in a month. *High school reunion.* Don't you get goosebumps just thinking about it? You look at yourself in the mirror. Have you gotten older? Ten . . . twenty . . . thirty years . . . What have you accomplished so far in your life?

You'll be able to see and speak with her again, the object of your affection, to whom you wrote love letters and sent roses and Serg's Chocolates. And you'll have to listen to some classmates who are full of hot air.

"Hey, man. How are things going?"

(You have yet to answer the question when he starts babbling away . . .)

"Me? I'm the General Manager of blah-blah-blah . . . "

And his monologue goes on. He gloats about his achievements, like a walking résumé. Everything you hear means more or less the same thing. "I'm amazing!" "My goodness, I'm a rich man!" "I look so fine!" "My car's interior smells like the Central Bank's." "I'd miss golfing three times a week if I were kidnapped today." "How much are you worth again?"

(At that point, you consider not attending the reunion at all.)

Reunions are pretty much like those "Time's up! Submit your papers, finished or not finished!" moments in school. Now was the time to be judged for who you've become and how much you're worth. Who turned out successful? Who turned out the "most" successful?

People say those who go to reunions are the ones who've got something to brag about. Why is it that people prefer tooting their horns to having genuine conversations after such a long time apart? What would happen if we told each other the truth?

"Hey, Bud! How are you?"

"Not too good, I lost my job at the factory."

"Well, you know, I'm the CEO of a multinational telecommunications company that specializes in yadda yadda yadda . . . Bill Gates may just be a smidgen richer than me."

"Oh wow! That's really something. I didn't even make it to college and I'm just living with relatives. Who is Bill Gates again?"

WHAT DO MANY YEARS OF STUDYING amount to? It's easy to see why we need money, but I don't understand why it must be the yardstick of success. Between the ages of twenty-one and sixty, we work for a living. From the ages of four to twenty-one, we attend school so that we can eventually find work. When we first start school, our bodies lack strength. When we retire, our bodies will have become feeble. We leave home as soon as the light begins to rise. We return home as the sun is setting. That is, after all, the way life is. If the only goal of studying is to get a job and earn a living, it's unsurprising that many people die in ignorance. Man has forgotten his holiness; he has forgotten that he is more than his academic Transcript of Records; that he is capable of more than what is listed on his résumé. His worth is greater than the amount on his payslip each payday.

What is intelligence precisely? Is it measured by A, B, C, D, F, 1, 2, 3, 5, P (Pass), F (Fail), 100%, 60%, 75%, O (Outstanding), S (Satisfactory) or NI (Needs Improvement)?

Who is smart? The best in spelling? Best in math? First Honor? Valedictorian? Magna Cum Laude? Board Exam Topnotcher?

Who is stupid?

Dyspraxia, dysgraphia, dysphasia and dyslexia are, respectively, an inability to correctly move the lips and tongue when speaking; difficulty controlling the fingers when writing; difficulty in speaking or understanding what others are saying; and difficulty comprehending the written word.

Who are the learning-disabled? Are they those who struggle with studying or those who have never learned anything at all?

What is the difference between a high-school dropout shoplifter and a Harvard-educated corrupt official, apart from the fact that the latter is wealthier?

Is the university professor with a master's degree who was in recent news for milking his students of money and harassing them sexually, considered competent? Is the principal who inflates school funds considered intelligent? Are cybercriminals and virus programmers geniuses?

Isn't it a grave mistake to allocate 10% for character, 20% for periodic tests, 30% for projects and 40% for class standing in the computation of grades,[43] when character is what shapes a person, a family, a country and the history of the world?

---

43 During my time.

I WAS GIVEN TEN CENTS for pocket money when I was in kindergarten. It was raised to seventy-five cents in first grade and the amount went up to ten pesos in sixth grade. It ranged from twenty to thirty pesos in high school. In college, my daily allowance was fifty.

Did I learn anything?

My registration cards indicate that 68,872.42 pesos was paid for my high school and college admission fees. My parents paid up to 6,600 pesos for various miscellaneous fees, books and school supplies during my seventeen years of school. Combined with my pocket money, the entire cost of my education came to 150,000 pesos.[44] That amount may appear to be peanuts nowadays, but it meant blood, sweat and tears back then.

Did I learn anything?

Counting all the hours I spent studying, I was in school for more than two years and sat in a classroom for 729 days. Additionally, I spent 5,100 hours on homework, projects, reviews and extracurricular activities. Plus, I believe I squandered around 56 minutes praying for class cancellations or wishing my professor would skip class.

---

44 Around $4,000 US dollars.

Did I learn anything?

I visited the Magnolia Dairy Plant, the Central Bank Security Printing Plant, Rizal Park, Rizal Shrine, Quezon Memorial Circle, Ninoy Aquino Parks and Wildlife Center, Nayong Pilipino Cultural Park, Mount Makiling, Vistamar Beach Resort, the Wax Museum, Fort Bonifacio, Tala Leprosarium and Bicutan Rehabilitation Center. I got vaccinated, went to confession, collected horse dung to make fertilizer in agriculture class, cooked menudo and "menudo-afritada fusion" for practical arts, dissected frogs for biology, did push-ups in Citizen Army Training, visited depressed areas for theology, oversaw the Registration of Voters for the Reserve Officers' Training Corps and took part in the Fun Run and Alay Lakad Walkathon.

Did I learn anything?

I attended six schools and enrolled 24 times. I participated in two graduation ceremonies, 12 Christmas parties, 8 field day demonstrations, 32 first-Friday Masses, about 1,140 flag raising ceremonies and Patriotic Oaths, took part in 960 exercise drills, had 2,400 recesses, 620 flag retreat ceremonies and countless embarrassing moments.

Did I learn anything?

I learned the life stages of a butterfly, different types of clouds and cell parts.

I learned about the caste system, mixed fractions, cradles of civilization, the 9th Symphony, the Trojan War, Bahay Kubo and the Three Little Kittens. I became acquainted wtih Whitman, Hitler, Newton, Lam-ang, Mozart, Naismith, Hamlet, Antonio Luna and Queen "Bloody" Mary.

I studied market segmentation, religious orders, business reports, military organization, as well as program documentation.

I learned to use a dictionary, encyclopedia, almanac, protractor, compass, watercolors, microscope, calculator and computer.

I learned to copy from others in exams and have others copy from me. I realized that the person who copies could end up getting a better score.

I realized it was wrong to constantly provide writing paper for bloodsucking classmates who refused to buy their own paper even if they had the money.

I learned that if you were lost in contemplation while walking, you could end up in the wrong classroom.

I learned that if you glanced at the floor while your finance professor was giving a lecture, you might find a hundred pesos.

I learned how difficult it was to finish a month-long project overnight.

I learned that calculus was . . . hold on. I don't know anything about calculus.

I learned that when you were caught in the rain without an umbrella, you could just buy a plastic bag from a street vendor. It was OK to play in the rain so long as your notebooks and books were wrapped in plastic. I learned that field trips should be canceled during a typhoon or heavy rain because you could end up being stranded in the flooded streets of Metro Manila until two in the morning.

I learned it wasn't good to be absent often because you could end up missing in the class photo.

I learned how fortunate I was to not, even once, have

my name misspelled in yearbooks and the list of graduates.

I learned that even if you thought you were the stupidest in geometry, you could still end up coming first in the exam. You should never underestimate your chances for good fortune.

I learned that it's better to have your notes up to date because some teachers will check your notebook out of the blue. And there are those who love giving surprise quizzes, so it's much better if you've read up on those notes.

In Boy Scouts I learned that it is important to always "be prepared."

I learned that it's possible to lose a classmate to death, no matter how young you are.

I learned that the world, in real life, is not the colorful murals seen in preschools. It doesn't always have a rainbow, sun, birds, trees and flowers.

I realized how fortunate I am to have parents who allowed me to play and who invested in my education. Not every child gets the chance to be a child.

I learned that as you grow older, you will stumble many times. Whether you get up again or not, life will go on, the world will turn and time will pass.

I learned that exams, school projects and quizzes are too trivial to ruin your life. And that it is a huge mistake to put your dreams aside just to avoid "terror teachers" and difficult subjects.

I learned that life is not a test with a pass mark. Life isn't a multiple-choice, identification, true or false, enumeration or fill-in-the-blanks type of test, but an essay written daily. It will not be judged based on right or wrong answers but on its meaningfulness or lack of it. Erasures are allowed.

I learned that life offers a plethora of free lectures and the syllabus is entirely up to you. There are many teachers available outside of school; you get to decide on who you will learn from. We are all enrolled in university, many subjects are challenging, but because it is free, you end up the loser if you drop out. We all will graduate eventually but in different ways. Our only diploma is the memory of whatever help we offered or the love we left in the world we once hoped to change.

I HAD INTENDED to go back to visit my high school for the longest time but plans kept fizzling out. But one day, after ten years of walking past the school campus, my feet could no longer stop me from entering the gates. Perfect, I thought. The school was on break and there weren't many people around. And because I still hadn't gotten my diploma, I thought of using that as an excuse should the security guard ask me about the purpose of my visit. But the guard paid me no mind. He was busy badgering the student whose ID was not pinned on his shirt I found the situation laughable. Things hadn't changed.

My school was located on a large campus. My heart raced as I approached the building. I recalled walking the path years before, lugging a large backpack, and rushing to make it to the flag ceremony on time.

I thought of my friends in the second year as I passed by the school canteen. We were dubbed the "Baon[45] Gang" because we always carried packed lunch in our bags. Whenever it rained heavily, the AM radio played loudly in the canteen, everybody awaiting the announcement of the suspension of classes.

The back of the high-school building was entirely different. There were more benches now, new and beautiful.

---

45 Packed lunch.

There were more plants as well. It was here we used to practice for group presentations. Here, we were ordered to pick dry leaves when the practical arts teachers went on a power trip. And it was also here that we searched for worms that we could torture when we ourselves were on a power trip.

The interiors of the high-school building remained unchanged. My beloved school was as worn down as ever, though nobody noticed because of the yearly paint jobs to cover up the writing on the walls. I recall how the Citizen Army Training commander reacted upon reading what someone wrote on the wall of the boys' restroom. "So what if you've seen Miss Garcia's enormous _____?" he said. "Did you really need to scribble it on the wall?"

Where I came from, everybody had a sense of humor.

I circled the whole building while the entire building circled my mind. I saw the library where I had to engage in a sword duel with the fire-breathing librarian before I could take out a book. I checked the biology room, where the display cabinets were still filled with shells and dead animals. I peeked into the music room; the piano was missing: the teacher must have thrown it at the students who sang out-of-tune. I saw the computer lab, which did not exist in our time. I walked through all the classrooms, even imagining myself sitting in one of the chairs.

I was nervous while I walked about, afraid that a teacher would call me out, ask me what section I belonged to and report me to my adviser. But there were no teachers. I was alone, after all. It was quiet, deafeningly quiet.

I went to the lobby to pick up the diploma at the registrar's office. The registrar was delighted to meet a former student. She answered my queries and then spent what seemed like half an hour telling me every single thing she knew that had happened since I graduated: classmates who turned out successful in their own fields, teachers who had left, some who'd got married and some who'd already passed on.

Before heading home, I decided to rest a bit on the steps of the quadrangle stage. This was where our class used to spend free periods. I couldn't help but feel nostalgic. I wondered where my classmates were now, after exchanging all those autographs, photos, hugs and kisses on graduation day. What happened to our fears and aspirations? Did they still laugh the way we used to? Were my teachers in good health? How could I possibly have thanked them if I only recently grasped what they had taught me?

When I left the high-school building, I noticed other new buildings that hadn't been there before. They were built in an area that used to be full of trees. Our favorite spot had been scrapped. Gone were the dry leaves, wet grass, hairy caterpillars and bird droppings. Gone were the memories of the camaraderie and bonds formed by that group of children who got to know the world all at the same time.

I carried home mixed feelings of joy and sadness. Since I now had my diploma, it was probably my last visit to the place that sheltered the dreams of my youth.

I'd gone back in time, but I couldn't make time turn back.

Foreword to the New Edition[46]

*(which I prefer to treat as just another
of the book's stories)*

EVEN BEFORE THIS BOOK HIT THE STORES in the Philippines, I did make another visit to my school to express my gratitude to my former teachers. They acknowledged my achievements and congratulated me on finally developing a personality (Yay!).

I also went to another school not to visit but to study. Just a short course in electronics. As a result, I am now capable of tinkering with broken appliances. They are still broken after I finish tinkering with them, but that's fine. What matters is that I gave studying and being in a happy class another shot. If only we could experience school on repeat loop. It feels fantastic. You leave home in the morning to pursue learning. When you get home in the afternoon, you turn out smarter than you were in the morning. Isn't that wonderful? Life after school is quite different. It's not always easy to remember that each day presents a new lesson to be learned. The tragedy is that people live their lives unaware of this truth.

Was I able to review and revise the entirety of this book? Is this all that I've learned? Is this book any better than it

---

46 This book was first published in the Philippines in 2001, and the new edition was published in 2013.

was in 2001 when it was first published? I'm not sure. Individuals and perspectives evolve. I may correct my errors, but I am still not perfect. My stories may have been more enjoyable and amusing when I first wrote them, but I cannot confine my mind to that time. While it is certainly more pleasant to just look back innocently on memories of youth, I cannot claim real education if I deny the lessons of the past and fail to appreciate the wisdom gained as an adult.

Amid my problems in college, there were several professors who exemplified conduct that was inappropriate for a respectable profession. It was an issue that society was just beginning to address at that time. Unwelcome behavior of a sexual nature which made young people feel even more uneasy about the world they were trying hard to figure out. We didn't know better then. I didn't. It was long after I left school that I understood the violation of ethics committed. And if I struggled with the intimidating and offensive learning environment during my time, I wonder how students involved in grave cases of sexual harassment or molestation like those in the news managed? Is the increase in the reported cases of abuse by teachers because of more extensive media coverage or is there truly more abuse occurring now?

What if, on the other hand, it was a teacher tormented with personal crises, who just happened to be in the wrong place at the wrong time, inopportunely caught on camera, and the footage went viral online? Things like this, along with the recurrence of school shootings in US and Europe, and reports of students setting fire to school equipment in protest about inadequate education funding, remind me of something I've long learned: unlike preschool murals, the real world does not always include a rainbow, sun, birds, trees and flowers.

They say that an effective story brings tears to the reader's eyes. On the contrary, I believe a story is a success when it brings tears to the author's eyes. I did not expect that revisiting these stories could still make me cry. It's difficult to be emotionally detached when recounting happy and not-so-happy memories—while thinking back on life and answering the question, "What did I learn and how did I learn from it?"

I am humbled by the boy who first wrote this book. He and I are different and I know it entailed great resolve for him to tell this story. I feel guilty at times when I think that I am not fully able to continue what he started.

When my book first went on sale in the Philippines, it was nearly rejected by a major bookstore chain since both the publisher and the author were unknown. Several members of the academic community criticized it as a poor example of literature and a bad influence on young people. It felt like a teacher had yelled at me and hurled back at me the school project I had put so much work into.

"Books choose their authors," Salman Rushdie said. This book, which I didn't bother to enter into any competition or to defend against critics, picked me. Despite its flaws, I wanted to justify and be proud of what this book has done for the arts, education, publishing industry and reading culture of the Filipinos. Some suggested including reviews and praises from celebrities on the cover like other books do. It's time it got the credit it deserves. Somehow.

Everything changed the moment I opened a handwritten letter I received in the mail one day. I wondered why the sender didn't just email me. I was surprised to know that it was from an overseas Filipino worker. He introduced himself, told me about his life, his family and his daily routine and said he only wanted to thank me for writing the book that kept him going and in good company while in prison in Taiwan. I felt emotional after I read the letter. I realized the significance of what I had started in 2001 and the value of sharing and empathizing with others through sincere storytelling.

There are people who read my books. I continue to learn more about life from them, and them from me. What more could I possibly ask for?

I would like to express my gratitude to you who, at this moment, are reading this book. No other recognition or testament to success comes close to the fact that you have chosen to read my work. I am humbled by your interest in my stories.

GOODBYE and thank you.

Those were the words we said in high school after class, a mechanical gesture, whether we'd slept through the lecture or if the teacher had spent the entire time scolding us.

I still remember seventy-five of my former teachers, while I fail to recall around ten. I am grateful to all of them, particularly my first-grade teacher, who taught me about faith (she was a devout Christian); my second-grade teacher, who spanked me without me knowing why; my third-grade teacher, who was a model teacher and was always diligent at her job; my fifth-grade teacher, who loved to shout in class; and my fourth and sixth-grade teachers, who were both excellent.

(There's more.)

To my first-year high-school adviser, who posted bail for me and my friend, Ulo; to my sophomore adviser, who taught the Baon Gang all about power tripping with worms behind the high-school building; to my third-year adviser, who demonstrated humility despite being the subject of petty rumors; and to our fourth-year adviser, who chose to put our many blunders aside and attended our last Christmas party in high school.

(Just a little more.)

To the English teacher who was always generous with praise and inspiration; to my social studies teacher who, despite being a terror, trusted me enough to have me represent our class in the Juniors team and compete in the United Nation's Day General Information Quiz Show;[47] to the terror math teacher in fifth grade who chucked shoes at students (I wasn't in that class); to that fifth-grade terror teacher who hurled not only shoes but blackboard erasers too (I was in that class) and to the music teacher who had no need for shoes or erasers and instead used the severed heads of noncompliant students to fling at other noncompliant students for maximum terror effect.

If parents with only a few children often run out of patience, imagine how much more difficult it is for teachers who handle classrooms of children every day? I'm OK with teachers being strict, as long they don't go overboard.

Like this former teacher who enforced only one rule in class: "Laziness is not tolerated here." The rule was clear, we knew what the repercussions were. We put all our laziness aside and studied hard . . . and learned a lot!

Teachers unintentionally teach their students a lot. Students unknowingly learn a lot from their teachers. "A teacher affects eternity; he can never tell where his influence stops." I sincerely thank my teachers and school for all the lessons, good, bad or ugly, that weren't part of the lesson plan and weren't covered by the miscellaneous school fees I paid.

---

47 We beat the Seniors team <*coughs*>

TO MY ELEMENTARY SCHOOL FRIENDS who taught me how to slip through barbed wire fences with the No Trespassing sign around farm areas.

To my high-school friends who taught me how to eat at the college canteen where dissected mammals used by college students lay on the table next to ours.

To my college pals who taught me to drink beer at room temperature and to sing while walking down the street.

To my friends at various schools who taught me that transferring to another school again and again is nothing to be ashamed of especially if you have no more hoots to give.

To my parents and siblings, who were my first teachers.

To my dear wife and kids who always inspire me to write masterpieces while also keeping me from getting work done.

To everyone who has read my work since 2001, especially those who have contributed to the improvement of this book and who have consistently shown their support for my advocacies.

To friends, coworkers, relatives, neighbors and countrymen who motivate me even when they are unaware of my existence.

To students who were happy and unhappy with their courses, schools, teacher, classmates and exam results but who remained resolute in confronting life and achieving their dreams.

And to the kind, eloquent and wisest Teacher who created Heaven and Earth.

THANK YOU SO MUCH.

(I seem to have forgotten something . . .)

Of course! Thanks also to my kindergarten teacher.

SERIOUSLY. WHEN I WAS A KID, I wanted nothing more than to work in a long-sleeved shirt and a tie when I grew up. If I ran into that kid today, I'm pretty sure I'd get yelled at. "Why didn't you become a waiter ?!"

Rewind.

Preschool was not common in those days. You were privileged if you attended kindergarten. I suppose I was, having attended kindergarten twice. There used to be little or no distinction between kindergarten, nursery, preschool and a day-care center. At least in my humble hometown, kids can attend "kindergarten," quit, and attend again when the child is older or more ready. It was structured as an almost informal education and was always adaptable to the needs of different families.

Our classroom, which was basically our barangay captain's[48] garage, was only a two-minute walk from our house. You had to bring your own chair and keep ten cents pocket money just in case you wanted to buy something at the canteen which was a small *sari-sari* neighborhood sundry store right across the street. School uniform was blue shorts and white shirt with DSWD[49] logo for the boys, and a jumper

---

48 The highest elected official in a *barangay*, the smallest level of administrative divisions of the Philippines.

49 The Department of Social Welfare and Development.

with the same specifications for the girls. Free snacks are distributed in the afternoons: porridge, *ginataan*,[50] or soup. Occasionally, we were also given free powdered milk and cornmeal, and were weighed regularly using a hybrid hanging scale which I can only describe now as something you'd mistake for a World War II torture device. It was intimidating and it led me to suspect that we might be sold on the meat market eventually or fed to a witch in some forest. Thankfully none of my fears came true and I learned many years later that this was the government's program to combat malnutrition in the country. We were under a dictatorship government, so it was very important that we looked healthy and happy and not as though we were under a dictatorship government.

Our school was a fun place. There were always people gathered about the room, watching. There wasn't much television in our area at the time, so our class served as the village's sports channel, soap opera channel and Discovery Channel.

Are you sleeping (2x)
Oh Bob Ong (2x)
Morning bells are ringing (2x)
Ding-dong-ding (2x)

When someone was about to nod off during a lesson, the entire class could be heard singing this song. It proved an effective way of rousing kids, who were shamed by the attention. Despite their bloodshot eyes, they would always do their best to participate.

---

50 A dessert made from coconut milk.

No one yelled nor got angry with anyone. Teachers weren't intimidating and they wouldn't coerce you to do anything. Nobody got a memo, or a suspension, or a bad record. That was kindergarten. Ruled by a mini government that was both effective and exemplary. Dignified and respectable. Most of the time.

IT ISN'T SOMETHING YOU EXPECTED. But you feel trouble growing inside you. Nobody knows and no one hears. You refuse to ask for help because there's no one who can help. One of life's bitter truths. It may be happening only now, but you know it could happen again anytime, anywhere, to anyone.

Do my classmates know? Perhaps not, they seem too preoccupied with writing their names over and over. Does my seatmate know? Maybe not, he appears to be taking his time coloring the houses, sun and trees on his paper. Does Teacher know? Maybe not, she seems to be busy watching over our other classmates. Nobody knows what you're going through or how much pain you're in right now.

You can't stand it anymore; you want to stop thinking; you want to end the suffering and pain. You don't care if you are mocked.

All you want is for the cold beads of sweat dripping from your body to stop. And you think . . . The time has come! You let go of the demon in your stomach. The dishonorable remains of food pushing their way out of your body. A split second passes. Only then are you able to breathe easily. The storm is over; the surroundings, peaceful. You feel like smiling but someone is threatening your happiness.

"What's that horrible smell?!"

A classmate dares expose the truth. You don't know who it is, but you want to curse him. Him and his big mouth.

You want to make him pay for his sin, when someone else chimes in.

"It really stinks!"

Huh?! Did you hear it right? There's more than one traitor in the class. And then another and another . . . they are growing in number. You are lost. Why does such a tragedy have to happen to an innocent child like me?

"Okay! Stand up, everybody. We shall dance and sing!"

Teacher ignores them; you are safe, but what is she asking you to do? How can you get up? How do you confess everything? Your eyes scan the area fast, your head turns, but your mother, sister or brother are nowhere to be found. Who do you turn to for help?

As your apprehension grows, you notice that all your classmates have their eyes on you, including Teacher. You are the only person seated. Everyone waits for you to rise from your chair; their gazes lock in on you. The entire class goes silent; your heartbeat is all that can be heard. You have no idea what else is out there for you. You contemplate not moving at all, but someone ends your suffering and breaks the silence.

"Oh, Teacher, he's pooped in his pants!"

Everything went black afterwards.

Despite the passage of time,
certain memories endure . . .

THE CLASS WAS CHAOTIC, as always. While she was away from her desk, I approached her seat with apprehension. Deftly, I took the note from my pocket, along with the bunch of tiny flowers and placed it in her school bag. Mission accomplished. Now I could relax and take a deep breath.

The following day, after class, I noticed a letter in my bag. I was certain it was from her. I could hardly wait to get home. When I got to my room, my hands were shaking as I opened the scented paper folded in three. Stars twinkled at the first glance of her handwriting. She said hi and proceeded to say my letter surprised her and delighted her at the same time. She told some stories. She made me laugh. And toward the end, a message that made my world go round, written in bold colored letters: I LOVE YOU.

In my head OMD's "Secret" was playing at full volume. I fell on the bed with my feet still on the floor, my hands outstretched, my palms open and the letter resting on my chest. My eyes rolled into nothingness. I traveled around the world and bounced through the clouds in just one heartbeat. If I had died then, I would have died smiling.

Being a charmer is something I probably got from Jose Rizal, who apart from being a Renaissance man, is also known as a ladies' man. In school, there was always someone that

189

I liked. From the first week of school, I immediately knew who my "inspiration" was. I had no qualms about approaching timid girls. I wasn't a hasty suitor, but I also wasn't a slacker. If I felt something for someone, I'd make sure to let the person know. Even if I only had one chance or if I had to wait for my chance to come. And I never cared where it would all end up or what I could get out of it. I just wasn't very good at hiding my feelings. But I did it in such a way that I would not be feared, resented or pitied as a result.

It's wonderful to fall in love and I've had plenty of opportunities to do so both in and out of school. But I never rushed, forced or abused it.

I knew there didn't have to be any other "firsts" in addition to first love. It's not fun to have "puppies" emerge from puppy love. And forget about "multiplying" if you're not yet an added source of income for your own parents.

(Please do not create a cover or an acoustic version of OMD songs and/or use it in a rom-com formula. Don't pick up love quotes out of context. Most importantly, if you haven't finished school or have projects due tomorrow, don't bother yourself with relationships just yet.)

So, what became of the letter? We'll continue the lesson next meeting. Class dismissed. <*wink*>

"Books to Span the East and West"

Tuttle Publishing was founded in 1832 in the small New England town of Rutland, Vermont [USA]. Our core values remain as strong today as they were then—to publish best-in-class books which bring people together one page at a time. In 1948, we established a publishing office in Japan—and Tuttle is now a leader in publishing English-language books about the arts, languages and cultures of Asia. The world has become a much smaller place today and Asia's economic and cultural influence has grown. Yet the need for meaningful dialogue and information about this diverse region has never been greater. Over the past seven decades, Tuttle has published thousands of books on subjects ranging from martial arts and paper crafts to language learning and literature—and our talented authors, illustrators, designers and photographers have won many prestigious awards. We welcome you to explore the wealth of information available on Asia at **www.tuttlepublishing.com**.

Published by Tuttle Publishing, an imprint of Periplus Editions (HK) Ltd.

www.tuttlepublishing.com

Library of Congress Cataloging-in-Publication Data is in process.

ISBN: 978-0-8048-5521-1

First edition
25 24 23 22   5 4 3 2 1

Printed in China   2211CM

Distributed by

North America,
Latin America & Europe
Tuttle Publishing
364 Innovation Drive,
North Clarendon,
VT 05759-9436, USA
Tel: 1 (802) 773 8930
Fax: 1 (802) 773 6993
info@tuttlepublishing.com
www.tuttlepublishing.com

Asia Pacific
Berkeley Books Pte. Ltd.
3 Kallang Sector #04-01
Singapore 349278
Tel: (65) 67412178
Fax: (65) 67412179
inquiries@periplus.com.sg
www.tuttlepublishing.com